FAT
A Life Unfiltered

FAT
A Life Unfiltered

Jon Stanton

John; J.B. -

Thanks for your
friendship and encouragement.

Blessings!

Jon Stnh

Cover Design by Sonjai Persaud, www.sonjaipersaud.com

Author Name:
Jon Stanton
Visit my website at www.hopefortheheavy.com

Printed in the United States of America

First Printing: November 2019

ISBN: 9781700341464

Acknowledgements

I've lost track of how many people have told me "write a book!" But a few people have played an especially important role.

First, my wife Janet, to whom words of thanks here would never convey the depth of my gratitude. Thanks for being my biggest fan, for listening, for encouraging, for supporting. I love you so much.

My friend and mentor, Jodi Davis. Thanks for helping me lose weight, sticking with me when I gained, and never stepping back from supporting me, regardless of my size.

My sister, Becka. Thanks for helping me in the earliest days of trying to lose weight and for offering feedback on this book.

Cindy Conger, of JustWrite Communications. Thanks for supporting my dream and for your editing skills.

Kathy Haake, Chicago Style guru extraordinaire, thank you for answering my questions and helping with style.

Kathy Wiens, thank you for taking time to review the final version of the manuscript.

Toni Jefferies, thank you for reviewing marketing materials and assisting with media.

Sonjai Persaud, thanks for designing such an awesome cover! Check out Sonjai's work at sonjaipersaud.com.

Lou White, thanks for helping me figure out how to publish this thing and for encouraging me to keep going when I felt like I was going to drown in the details.

Table of Contents

Big Wheel   1

Glue Girlfriend and Other Love Stories   7

Love and Marriage   23

Carland   37

Donuts   49

I'm German – I'll Eat Anything with Sausage, Noodles
    or Type 2 Diabetes   57

That's Gonna Leave a Mark   69

Maintenance, We Have an Emergency   79

Planes, Trains and Automobiles   93

Baseball, Hot Dogs, Revival Meetings, and Heart Disease   111

Photos   125

Does Skin Tone Come in Lobster?   133

Gym Class and Other Terrifying School Experience   149

Clothes   165

Skin and Other Bodily Changes   179

Job and Career   193

God Must Hate Me Because I'm Fat   203

Yo-Yo Hell   219

Denial and Truth   225

Inspiration   243

Foreword

I sat down at my desk before sunrise on a crisp fall morning in 2012 and began writing. At the time, I was newly married, had moved to a different state for the first time in more than two decades, had quit a job I'd been in for more than ten years, and was desperately trying to squelch a growing waistline and a downhill slide into despair as a result of gaining weight.

I was also trying to write that book that everyone had been telling me to write since losing 230 pounds without surgery between 2007 and 2009. But I was trapped in an oxymoron, trying to figure out how to inspire while once again fearing that I might expire if I did not do something about my weight. The slow creep upward had already begun...again.

Fast forward to the present, and here I am sitting at my desk, still happily married, living in another different state, having recently quit my job, and still desperately trying to squelch that waistline that grew exponentially in the past seven years and has once again put my life in danger. And I've decided it was time to finish that book that had been sitting "out in the cloud" of cyberspace for several years.

I've written this book for two primary reasons. First, I love to make people laugh, and my hope is that many of the stories you find within will do exactly that. Being the funny guy in the room makes people like and accept you when you fear they will reject you because of your size.

Laughter is also cathartic. There's a reason many psychologists place emphasis on the importance of being able to laugh at yourself. Laughter heals, both physically and emotionally. Making people laugh is still one of my more common coping mechanisms, but with time, I've come to realize that I enjoy making people laugh because I enjoy seeing people happy.

Second, my goal is to help you – regardless of your physical size – understand the life and emotional pain of those who struggle with weight. Being one hundred pounds or more overweight hurts. There is physical pain, but the emotional hurt is more devastating.

Hopefully, you will come to understand from my own journey and the stories of many people who've had similar life experiences, that our weight problem is not just about eating too much. It's more about WHY we eat so much, and much of that has to do with what's going on in our heads more than in our bodies.

Welcome to the world of the ever-increasing portion of the population in the U.S. who are more than one hundred pounds overweight and have been this way most of their lives. I wrote this book, in part, to tell our stories through my story. I've been privileged to talk with hundreds of people who have struggled with being morbidly obese, and universal themes have emerged out of those discussions. My story is likely very similar to your story or the story of someone you love and care about.

So, while this book had auspicious beginnings as an attempt to inspire others that they could lose weight and have the healthy life they had always wanted also, it's now morphed into a quasi-memoir peppered with stories from a unique life, along with a healthy dose of inspiration.

I grew up in a pastor's home, which meant living in many places and interacting with many people. Our family lived in a fishbowl of scrutiny, but with my enjoyment of observing the world around me and people-watching, I was a fish that stared right back. You will see my weight as an oft-present actor in these vignettes and stories from my life. Like the proverbial elephant in the room (almost literally, for once), it's always with me.

Some final words before we begin. The stories you are about to read are based on real people and real events but may not be completely accurate. Consider this your warning for when my book makes it to Oprah! Some of the stories took place a long time ago, so I'm relying on distant memories. Others may have been embellished or changed due to my nature as a storyteller; some of the parties involved may have a different take on the actual events. I've changed names to protect the innocent... and the guilty.

Also, I've made it a bit of a personal mission to redeem the word "fat." You'll see that I use it frequently and descriptively throughout. Please don't be offended. Fat is not a dirty word, but it's been made out to be that way because of people who choose to use it hurtfully. I try to avoid silly, overly-politically correct adjectives like "pleasingly plump" or "big boned." I'm fat. Maybe you are, too. It's OK to say so.

Last, please note that this book is not set up chronologically and there is not one, singular cohesive plot. Each chapter is a story unto itself, and some things may be repeated in more than one spot.

There are many stories to tell from my life; stories to make you laugh, cry, and perhaps inspire a change in your life. Through it all, I hope you will be motivated to consider your own story and your preferred future. In the grand scheme of things, life is pretty brief. Live it to the fullest.

PART 1

You'll Laugh

"To truly laugh, you must be able to take your pain
and play with it."
— Charlie Chaplin

1

Big Wheel

By all accounts, I was born "normal," arriving in this world at slightly more than eight pounds, and about twenty-one inches long. It wouldn't take long for that first number to increase to the "abnormal" range. The ramifications took their toll by the time I was two and encountered my first Big Wheel.

For those of you unfamiliar with this moment in American history, the Big Wheel was basically a large, plastic tricycle with one significant modification. Much like those fancy recumbent bikes that allow senior citizens to continue pedaling well into their golden years, the Big Wheel's seat was close to the ground, and the pedals were out in front of you in the center of a giant, plastic front wheel. Two fat plastic wheels sat behind the rider.

The Big Wheel came in all sorts of colors. My Big Wheel, which I shared with my older brother, Dave, was red, yellow and blue, with black highlights.

The body was bright red and had a decal along the side declaring your pride as the owner of a Big Wheel. Or maybe that was there to identify the mangled heap left after one of the many Big Wheel accidents during that era when the streets of small towns were overrun with unlicensed, toddler Big Wheel drivers. I understand that no-fault policies were available, but the state did not require Big Wheel insurance, so few people had it.

The adjustable seat was bright blue. It had three positions. Skinny kid, normal kid and fat kid. What was missing was the morbidly obese, big and tall kid position. For those of us over the weight limit of seventy pounds, this created a conundrum. How does a fat kid or a tall kid ride a Big Wheel? Keep in mind, too, that the Big Wheel was recommended for ages two to eight. I was two years old and already over the weight limit. What was I going to do? My solution was to take the seat out completely and hang my butt off the back of the Big Wheel. It worked, and as a two-year-old, I didn't even think about how silly it must have looked.

The front wheel and steering column of the Big Wheel were a sight to behold. The large wheel, yellow on my model with black, triangular accents and an outer ring of black with durable non-steel-belted radial ply technology, was made entirely of plastic. The steering column was modeled after the latest Harley-Davidson, with dual plastic grips.

If you were lucky and your parents had money, customizable fringes were available for the ends of your grips. Fake stickers that looked like gauges were provided. My model had no brakes; later models added a hand brake to one of the back wheels that usually resulted in a major spinout when desperately trying to keep yourself from crashing into the tree at the bottom of the hill. Power was provided by two Plasti-Steel pedals and two skinny, normal or chubby legs.

Neighborhood Big Wheel races were common, although the races in which I participated often devolved into demolition derbies. My brother was especially astute and speedy on the Big Wheel, a source of contention in our relationship. I was more concerned with adequate Big Wheel upkeep, whereas he was happy to participate in the demolition derbies often arriving home with a dented front wheel. He also neglected to keep the Big Wheel safely garaged at night, leaving it haphazardly on its side in the driveway where it was at risk of a vehicle drive-over or being stolen. I protested loudly to my parents, but he still got away with Big Wheel abuse.

For me, a typical ride in my early days included lots of screaming and yelling as I soared down our Michigan driveway's steep hill, unhelmeted, at unsafe speeds. The goal was to spin out or negotiate a hard turn into the yard before flying out into oncoming traffic on the road in front of our house. The Big Wheel also lacked seatbelts or airbags and my parents, never overly concerned with safety issues, didn't consider helmets. Of course, no other parents did either. It was the era of helmet-free living and head-injuries galore.

Over time, we also discovered the Big Wheel had two fatal flaws, outside of the lack of brakes or warning labels regarding damaged heads. The first was related to those "durable non-steel-belted radial ply technology" front wheels I mentioned earlier. The marketers lied; the wheel was not durable.

In the course of a year, our Big Wheel developed a giant hole in its front tire. Lacking an odometer, I'm unable to provide a sense of its mileage at the time, but this ever-enlarging hole would eventually pick up stones which would rattle around inside the wheel making the most annoying sound. Occasionally, one of the stones would mount an escape and come hurtling out of the tire hole hellbent on inflicting damage to something or someone upon its freedom. My brother and I secretly hoped this would happen when one of our sisters was in firing distance, but it was impossible to time.

The Big Wheel's second fatal flaw involved its chassis, or maybe it was a suspension issue. I was never quite sure and couldn't get a square answer from the neighborhood Big Wheel mechanic. All I know is that eventually, saggage became an issue, and when I was seatlessly perched on the rear of the Big Wheel, the back tires would bow out, and the chassis would drag on the ground.

This eventually led to a chewed-up floor pan, and a tremendous amount of teasing from neighborhood bullies. It didn't help matters that my brother, who used the skinny seat setting, had no such problems. Even at this early age, I was becoming painfully aware that my weight made me different and a target for bullies.

One day, I headed down the driveway with a larger than usual amount of gusto, and nearing the road with oncoming traffic, I decided to execute a quick turn to the right. Due to my great velocity, however, it became readily apparent I had exceeded the Big Wheel's operational capacity.

As I began to career at a high rate of speed, there was a sickening snap as both back wheels broke and went flying off in opposite directions. I slammed down hard on the ground and quickly flipped to the left, finding myself in a rollover crash of magnanimous proportions. Helmetless, as usual, I was lucky that I had flipped onto a grassy part of the hill, and other than the rocks flying out of the hole in the Big Wheel's front tire, I was no worse for wear.

My parents and my angry brother examined the remaining carnage of the Big Wheel. "Well, that's a goner," said my dad.

Always concerned about my weight, my mom asked her usual question when something I was using broke, ripped or was otherwise destroyed. "What did you eat for lunch?" she said.

My brother just glumly shook his head.

I was not yet three years old, so that meant I was basically wailing and crying my head off, more concerned with the boo-boo on my knee than the destruction of the Big Wheel.

"That's going to leave a mark," said my dad.

It would be the first of many.

2

Glue Girlfriend and Other Love Stories

As I'm sitting here writing this chapter, I'm celebrating my seven-year anniversary. Seven years ago today, my blessed wife and I took the leap into the realm of the betrothed. It wasn't an easy journey getting to that day, and my wife (who could probably write a book of her own about the experience of being married to a fat food addict) deserves a thousand gold medals for taking a chance on me.

I have encountered a number of difficulties in the love department – many of these because of my weight and the related self-esteem issues. For someone such as me who has been fat since long before love interests even came on the radar, the pursuit of love has been a bizarre experience. If you have never been fat or ugly, you have no idea what it's like hoping that someone will actually give you a moment's notice. If you have been fat or ugly, you can probably relate to some or most of what I'm going to share.

I started dating when I was in first grade. I used kindergarten to hone my skills in selecting girlfriends. Based on my first choice the next school year, I must have needed more time to learn the ropes. My first girlfriend was indeed an interesting individual.

In the summer between kindergarten and first grade, my family moved from Illinois to Iowa. Our new home, a small town of about fifteen hundred people, was located about thirty miles from the state capital of Des Moines. Like most small towns in Iowa, the village boundaries were easy to identify.

Roughly the shape of a rectangle, the children of Dallas Center, Iowa, knew it was time to turn your bike around when you encountered one of four cornfields, which we helpfully labeled as Cornfields A through D. Cornfield D was also easily identifiable by the nearby Hyland Chicken Farm and the stench of chicken poo. Thus, we mostly avoided riding our bikes toward Cornfield D.

The church where my dad served as a pastor was located on the east side of town, just a few blocks from downtown and adjacent to one of the two city parks. My first girlfriend lived just around the corner from the church on the way up the hill toward Cornfield B.

It's altogether possible that I met her during that first summer when the neighborhood kids were outside all day, speeding around on bicycles or playing in the park. Atari Game Systems had just been invented, Nintendo was a word no one knew, and most parents, mine included, would never let their kids sit in the house all day staring at the television screen. Summers meant no school and being outdoors from sunup to sundown.

Once school started, I quickly realized that small town life meant that everyone basically knew everyone else outside of school, too.

My first-grade classroom was inside the high school. Apparently, an Iowa blizzard approximately six years prior had resulted in an especially large number of first graders. The nearby elementary school didn't have the capacity, so the first graders, divided into two adjacent classrooms, met in the high school. I suspect that my exposure to the high levels of teenage hormones and pheromones may have been what drove my desire to locate my first girlfriend as soon as possible.

I needed some criteria to get started, so I developed a list.

1. Female
2. Not already taken.
3. Not someone who one of the non-fat guys is likely to take.
4. Has at least a 48-count Crayola crayon box (not a knock-off brand) and a 24-ounce Elmer's glue (also not a knock-off brand).

I started making my list.

First up was Heather. I quickly discovered she only had a 24-count box of crayons, so she was out. I considered Charlotte next, but she was mouthy and always in trouble with the teacher. She did have a 64-count box of crayons, which made her especially interesting, but I didn't think I'd be able to handle her attitude.

After carefully analyzing each candidate against my criteria, I settled on Hayley. She could be a bit mouthy too, but the teacher seemed to still like her. Plus, she had the biggest bottle of glue I'd ever seen. I didn't even know Elmer's made one that size!

I quickly set about wooing her. I passed her notes with little hearts drawn on them when the teacher wasn't looking. I gave her one of my lunchbox cookies. I drew pictures of her during art time, which, in hindsight, it's amazing that didn't turn her off given my lack of artistic skills. Even my stick people looked deformed.

I also set about getting her friends to secretly tell her of my interest. She agreed to start seeing me casually. All seemed to be going in the right direction, but then a tragedy occurred.

You see, my first grade-school girlfriend was the class freak. It made sense that we hooked up (in that grade school kind of way) because I was the other class freak. My weight, along with being the preacher's kid, placed me high on the list of class freaks. Her placement on the list, unfortunately, was because she was slightly overweight and ate glue.

That was the tragedy. My first girlfriend ate Elmer's Glue! I don't think she huffed, since most kids in the 1980s didn't know about huffing glue, but she did eat it. I saw her. She thought it was cool. I found it intriguing. The teacher, and most others, thought it was completely gross.

Although I had seen her eat glue a couple times, I found out about her glue addiction one day during art time. The teacher passed out instructions for the day's project, which would include the use of our glue. How exciting it would be to see my girlfriend's oversized glue bottle once again! She had to keep it in her locker because it wouldn't fit in her desk.

She was bringing the bottle back to her desk when I heard the teacher say, "Hayley, what on earth have you done with all of the glue? Have you been eating it again?"

Hayley had a sheepish look, and her face turned bright red.

"No, I have NOT!" she said emphatically.

"Well then, what happened to it?" said the teacher. "We've talked about this many times before, and you and your parents agreed you weren't going to eat anymore glue. It's not good for you!"

A realization hit me that my girlfriend's big glue bottle wasn't because she was cooler than all the rest of us with our 24-ounce bottles. She was eating her glue way more often than I realized.

My intrigue morphed into horror. I thought she only ate glue occasionally. Now, with the large, half-empty bottle in sight, I envisioned a digestive system coated in Elmer's and a girlfriend eternally constipated. How could this be? I had no choice but to dump her. I quickly passed a note to Charlotte, her best friend, expressing my condolences. Hayley didn't speak to me for weeks.

Thus began a long saga in my life of unstable girlfriends. My second-grade girlfriend wanted to play doctor on our third or fourth date. I belonged to a conservative holiness church, and when she started to undress in the playhouse in her backyard, I hightailed it home sure that Satan himself was opening the trap door to hell *just* for me.

I did have a short and blessed reprieve in third grade, though. Elizabeth Busby had tantalizing pigtails. They hung there like oversized Twizzlers, and I was mesmerized. On top of that, Elizabeth was smart. Super smart. And she was a nerd. I was a nerd, too. Elizabeth and I hit it off over the common bond of our nerdiness and quickly became entangled in a wild love affair surrounded by our Apple II E computers.

In those early days at the dawn of the computer age, our school's newly acquired Apple II E computers were reserved for use only by the smart kids, or as the school liked to call us, "gifted and talented." We were the only ones allowed to leave the regular classroom a few times each week and instead learn how to program in the BASIC computer language on the Apple.

I was in awe of Elizabeth's computer skills. Most of our time was spent learning how to create drawings using plotting commands in BASIC. Always being better at words than art, I would choose a bright cheery magenta and spell out "You Compute Me" and then quickly show my creation to Elizabeth. She, on the other hand, was quickly programming the computer to create a multi-color mockup of the Taj Mahal. My jealously fanned the flames of my love interest even more.

Elizabeth was a tough one to unravel, though. She seemed more interested in what was happening with the stock market than spending time with me. I didn't give up easily. Gradually, I learned what topics were interesting to her, and I would go to the library on the weekend to read up on them so we could have an educated discussion in between plotting graphics in BASIC and playing "Where in the World is Carmen San Diego?" on the Apple II E.

All was going well, but then tragedy struck, again. My parents announced we were moving to Ohio and third grade would be my last in Iowa. Elizabeth and I promised to stay in touch, but as is so often the case with elementary school romances, we soon forgot about each other and didn't reconnect until the advent of Facebook. She's still a nerd and she still loves computers and economics. She's worked for Fortune 500 companies, and I am proud she is still my friend.

After moving and getting used to a new school, my track record of psychologically unstable choices recommenced. My fourth-grade girlfriend had to wear a long skirt in gym class for religious reasons but was also quick to beat up anyone who got in her face on the playground. I wasn't quite sure how to handle such a volatile personality, and that, coupled with my growing sense that other than Elizabeth, I had not had a very good track record, meant I pretty much swore off women by the time I was in fifth grade.

By this time, my weight had also expanded exponentially. I became so fat, and in my opinion, so ugly, that even the desperate girls would have nothing to do with me. From ages eleven to sixteen, I had no girlfriends. I was popular with the girls but in a completely unromantic way. My teenage self realized girls like nice guys, but they generally don't want to bond with them, emotionally or physically. I felt like most of the girls wanted a guy with some daring and gusto. I had neither. I was just nice. A nice nerd. A nice, fat nerd.

We returned to Michigan when I was in tenth grade. We had moved from there when I was three years old. This meant that all sorts of people knew me, but I hardly knew anyone. It was a strange experience. Being nice, however, I quickly made friends, and settled in. I was still a nerd, and although I had to avoid being beat up on a relatively frequent basis because I was fat and the preacher's kid, I was mostly able to enjoy school, especially after Kristie entered my world.

Kristie, whom you will read more about in other chapters, is my friend Jared's older sister. When I met her, she was attending Michigan State University working on a degree in art history. Kristie also attended my church.

She, along with Jared, his other siblings, and our friends Raylene and Brandy, became known as "The Carland Hounds," a nomenclature associated with the small town of Carland, where some of us lived or lived close by. We weren't the Bloods or the Crips, but we definitely had our own language, our own reputation, and our own code of commitment. In other words, we had each other's backs. You'll read more about the Carland Hounds later.

As time went on and as the Carland Hounds became a more fully integrated unit, I started to really enjoy being with Kristie. Kristie was the kind of person who almost always had a smile on her face. Even when she was upset, unless you knew her well, it was hard to tell.

Kristie had wheels and the power of the purse. She carried a lot of the workload for her large family. She helped her mom with a lot of the grocery shopping, laundry, and other household tasks, all while driving seventy miles each day to take classes at MSU, and somehow finding time to study.

I think Kristie may have eventually fallen in love with me because I kept her company, and helped with a lot of the tasks, too, especially laundry. We spent many happy hours at the Town Tub Laundromat in the nearby town of Elsie. We would both do our schoolwork in between cycles washing and drying. Over time, we realized how much we enjoyed being with each other.

Kristie seemed like the first normal woman to really give me the time of day, at least in the romance department. Of course, she didn't give me even that until I did some pretty heavy pursuing. There were two primary obstacles between us.

First, there was the age barrier. I was fifteen, and Kristie was twenty-one. I'm sure she hesitated to be known as the cradle robber and didn't want to deal with all the gossip that would ensue from having a relationship with me.

The town of Carland was also known for The Carland Cable Network. No, it wasn't Dish, Time Warner, or anything like that. It was a hotline of nosy grandmas engaging in daily gossip about anyone and anything that fulfilled their need for a little local soap opera. I was a primary topic for the Carland Cable Network because I was the pastor's son. You'll find out more about them in another chapter.

Our second obstacle was height. Kristie comes from a family of giants. She was six feet tall and big boned. She was a large woman, but not because of weight. She was just tall, and big. My grandma would have said she was designed to give birth. All I knew was that she had to stoop a little bit so I could kiss her. In my youthful obliviousness, I didn't pay attention to our age or height differences. Kristie read *Cosmo,* so she was probably more concerned than I was about dating someone five years her junior and almost three inches shorter.

Nevertheless, after a period of begging and wooing, Kristie gave in, and we became a couple. We were nearly inseparable after that. We continued to do household chores together, and traveled together, ate together, played together, prayed together, and just generally enjoyed being with each other. I loved buying Kristie small gifts with my meager pizza-shop income. Kristie was a trooper, and even though she was in college, she attended many of my high school activities. It must have been hard for her to be the only college student at the high school prom!

My friends thought I was unbelievably cool for having a college-aged girlfriend. I fielded frequent requests for liquor purchases. At that time in my life, I was a relatively pious person, so all requests were denied. My piety carried over into other areas of my life. Kristie and I would smooch on a regular basis, but we never moved beyond that because I was convinced that hell was right around the corner if we went any further before we were married. Kristie dutifully attended church with me, and my reputation as the pious preacher's son was mostly kept intact.

I can honestly say that in the years we were together, I don't recall Kristie ever saying anything about my weight. She was one of the few people in my life who didn't continually draw attention to what was my most notable feature. That might partly be because of love, but I think it's more likely it was because Kristie is just a genuinely nice person who doesn't prioritize a person's physical features when she forms a relationship with them. To her, it wasn't an issue. She loved me for me, not for what I looked like.

Of course, I am realizing all of this now in hindsight. At the time, I was reaching the point in my life of near total denial about my weight. Fat people must create and live in a world of total denial if they want to survive. It's an evolutionary defense mechanism, mostly. People (and especially men) who are normal and healthy use their brawn and good looks to obtain evolutionary dominance. Fat men have to deny the fact that they are near the bottom of the evolutionary chain, or they would likely just give up, curl up in the corner, and die. That, along with heart disease, would be the end of fat humanity.

I'm joking a bit, but the other reason that denial is so necessary is because fat people have a very hard time living with themselves. Psychologically it's necessary to convince yourself every day that your fatness doesn't define you, and that it's really not a problem. If you are fat, you know what I mean. If you have never been fat, think about some of the fat people you know, or some of the fat people on reality TV shows who deny that their fatness is killing them.

By the time Kristie and I were together, I had entrenched the denial of my fatness into my overall psyche in order to survive. By this time, most of the bullying and teasing that I had endured during elementary and middle school had ceased. I pretended that my weight had no bearing on my life. But deep down, I hated myself, I hated my body, and I was jealous of everyone around me who wasn't fat and didn't understand my pain.

So, my denial carried over into my relationship with Kristie. I suspect that Kristie probably had no idea how much I hated myself and how much I struggled with self-loathing and low self-esteem. I put on a very good front, even to the person to whom I was closest. Most people who knew me at this time in my life saw me as a person full of confidence who knew exactly what he was going to do in life. Nothing could have been further from the truth. I, like most fat people, excelled at wearing masks. If you have fat friends, they are most likely not expressing their genuine feelings. Fat people are masters of illusion.

I broke up with Kristie the month before I left Michigan to attend college in Ohio. I clearly remember the day. I was working at the pizza shop and had been ignoring her for several days. She came in to talk to me, and while I folded pizza boxes in the back room, I told her it was over. I used the excuse that I was leaving town and didn't want to maintain a long-distance relationship.

The truth was that Kristie was more like a sister to me, and I couldn't see myself being romantically involved with my sister. In hindsight, I realized that I had a tendency to use people to make myself feel and look better. I did love and have feelings for Kristie, but I knew early on that they weren't romantic feelings. I kept up the façade though, because she was fun, and it was cool to have an older girlfriend. Heck, it was cool to have a girlfriend PERIOD, because I had spent most of my youth convinced that no woman would ever have any interest in me.

A few years after we split, Kristie fell in love with a wonderful guy that I also knew quite well. I think he was a little wary of me at first, since the Carland Hounds still got together when everyone was in town and Kristie and I had remained friends. I took him aside, told him that I was so happy for them, and that he did not need to worry about me being a problem or issue in their relationship. I meant it, and I think he was relieved.

I ended up playing the piano for their wedding a couple of years later, and I have watched with great joy as they have built a family together. Kristie and her husband attended my wedding, too, and I was overjoyed.

Before I tell you about my awesome wife, I must first tell you about the desert season in between. I'm sure you are waiting on bated breath to hear the next chapter in my love life, but there is no chapter between Kristie and Janet. None, nada, nein.

There were no romantic relationships in my life for the next fifteen years. After breaking up with Kristie, I was an awful mess and decided not to take chances on relationships because I might get hurt. With a lifetime of enduring all sorts of hurts, I didn't want any more, convinced myself that Kristie was an unusual blessing, and that no other sane woman would EVER want to have anything to do with someone as fat and ugly as me. The barrier of all barriers went up, and I surrounded my heart with a wall several feet thick.

There were a couple of "interesting" women that came along during the desert period, but I successfully fended them off. Honestly, I couldn't fathom why these women wanted anything to do with me. I did have some sort of sick satisfaction in realizing that somehow, I attracted some women. One woman literally threw herself at me, and looking back on it now, I am completely perplexed.

Cheryle was a classmate during my stint in college working on an education degree. We had known each other beforehand through our jobs, so at first, I was thrilled to have someone in class that I knew pretty well. She was apparently thrilled, too.

Cheryle's bubbly personality attracted me. I also knew that she had a history that was rife with instability, and for that reason, she scared me a bit. She also had a good body, and I liked that about her, too. I was still wearing my persona of piousness, though, so I tried to not pay attention to that too much.

I was afraid of going to hell, so I would pray fiercely asking God to divert my attention with holy things and holy thoughts. "Purify my heart, let me be as gold, and precious silver..."

"If a man lusts in his heart, he…goes to hell," or at least that was my interpretation of the Bible. I think Cheryle noticed my distress.

My classmate, Char, also noticed my distress, and thought it was hilarious. Char attended my church and was a very good friend of our family. We hung out a lot together, as she was also single and had sworn off ever having a relationship again. We had a lot in common and loved to read, so even though it wasn't required for her degree, she signed up for the same literature course that Cheryle and I had to take as part of our education program.

We sat at tables, each with three seats, for our class. Cheryle always managed to sit directly between Char and me, giving Char a window into what was happening in my relationship with Cheryle.

Anyhow, I was pious and not a perv, so I continued to try and stay on the high road. Char continued to be amused. Cheryle finally had enough of my piousness and one evening she made her move.

Our class was on the second story of the building. Because I was fat and Cheryle was also plump, we used the elevator. As the door closed, Cheryle reached over and hit the emergency stop button. In one flash, she ripped off her shirt and moved toward me. I don't recall exactly what she said, but it was along the lines of, "If you want me, I'm yours! Take me right now."

Well, that didn't happen. I would like to say it was my desire to take the high road and save myself for marriage, but I wasn't even thinking about that at the time. The main consideration in my mind was that we were in an elevator, stuck between floors. If I had decided to go for it, I would have had maybe less than five minutes to lose my virginity before someone began to wonder why the elevator was taking so long.

Even more than that, my fear of hell completely paralyzed me. There was no chance that nature was going to take its course with all these stressful circumstances at play. The adrenaline was pumping. If you're in the medical profession, you know that adrenaline kills the hormones that are necessary for the physical reaction required to fornicate.

I was completely shocked and terrified; anything but aroused. I couldn't believe what was happening. I was at least seven years into my desert period, and I could not fathom that ANY woman would respond to me in this fashion. Truth be told, it would have been physically impossible to do the deed in that cramped elevator. I weighed more than 430 pounds. Cheryle was probably at least 200 pounds on a frame less than five feet tall. Under the laws of physics, vertical conjugation was not possible.

Most of that was not really on my mind at the time. What was on my mind was escape. What was I going to say and do to get out of this situation? I decided to take the spiritual route. Making someone feel guilty is a tried and true technique for defusing a sexually charged situation.

I was shaking as I quickly and quietly told Cheryle that I was a Christian, and that Christians don't have sex until they are married. Those who have sex before they are married go to hell, and I did not want to go to hell. I thought she was a nice person and I did not want her to go to hell either. To save us both from hell, I was going to pull the emergency stop button so that the elevator would run again, and we could make it to class on time.

Cheryle looked at me with total incredulity. She managed to get her shirt back on before the elevator reached the second floor, and we arrived at class just as it was starting. Char was waiting with a smile on her face and asked if we had taken too long eating our Little Debbie snack cakes in the cafeteria. Okay, I made that up, but I'm sure she had some smart remark.

During the break, I took Char aside and told her what had happened. She laughed, coughed, laughed some more, slapped me on the back, laughed some more, made some comment about how "irresistible I was to women," laughed some more, told me how proud she was of my commitment to Christian purity, and laughed even louder. This would be my last "interesting" experience for quite some time. After another season in the desert, God sent me the greatest blessing ever...my wife.

3

Love and Marriage

My wife and I are an electronic couple. We met each other, formed a relationship, and eventually married thanks to the Internet. We haven't been asked to make a commercial, but we are a Match.com success story. I like to joke that we were one click away from having never met each other.

The click in question belonged to my wife. After we were dating, she admitted that she had come very close to moving past my profile because she didn't really care for my picture. Being the type of person who is more interested in substance than in appearance, she went ahead and read my profile and was intrigued. Her fate was sealed when she went back to my pictures and clicked through to the second one, a photo of me at a baseball game that she liked much more. Whew!

Match.com was a very interesting experience for me. How do you sell yourself when you view yourself as nothing more than a squishy blob of Crisco trying to find love? How many women are really going to respond to "Stay-Puffed Marshmallow Man Seeks Life-Long Love for S'more-Like Experience?" Many fat people don't even try. It's true. I encountered very few fat women on Match.com.

When I first signed on to Match.com and eHarmony, I was near the lowest weight of my adult life. I had spent almost two years losing 230 pounds. From a physical perspective, I thought it was my best chance of finally catching a woman's attention and interest.

The first items that online dating sites require are a profile photo and a descriptive phrase. These hooks will be used to catch prospective suitors' attention. It's an agonizing process. I changed my profile picture and description often, usually after month-long periods of absolutely no interest from anyone.

I decided early on to avoid trite phrases like, "life-long love" because those make me want to barf. I had to come up with a way to describe myself that didn't include the negative thoughts that often ran through my head:

"Ugly former fat person with a stable income seeks woman interested in improving my self-worth."

"Geeky nerd seeks geeky nerd for Star Trek-like experiences."

"Deflated Pillsbury Doughboy looking for interesting biscuit for butter-melting times of love and fun."

"Are you interested in being involved with a completely useless human being? I'm your man."

Developing a good tagline is an exercise in futility, pain and hellishness when you don't value anything that you do bring to the table.

After a lifetime of never hearing anyone say anything even remotely positive about my physical appearance, I thought that maybe I could finally describe myself without alluding to my weight. It simply wasn't possible, though. My weight problem was at the center of my very being, and it was impossible to simply bypass it as some bygone issue. Plus, I decided that I needed to explain why I really did look like a deflated Pillsbury

Doughboy. It was quite obvious that someone or something had "pulled my plug."

I anticipated that I would receive so many winks (that's how people indicate they are interested in you on Match.com) that I would have a hard time keeping up. I was sure my weight loss had propelled me from zero to ten on the hotness scale and that women would be beating down the door to score a date with me.

After three winks in three months and virtually no response to any of my own winks, I realized that good looks were not my best marketing tool. I was going to have to sell myself through words, not photographs.

Well, words weren't a problem. As the king of verbosity, my profile page was already one of the wordiest on the entire Match.com site. I decided to fine tune it a bit, and...I decided to be honest. Novel concept, I know, but keep in mind that I never sought to date for more than a decade. I'm not a dishonest person, but I am a marketer, which means I know how to emphasize (or stretch) the positive and eliminate the negative.

I switched up the words in my profile. I cut down the longest description on the planet after realizing that wordiness turns off a lot of women. Apparently, men are supposed to be non-verbal. I missed that memo. Here is the final profile I used, with intermittent comments about what I wrote many years ago.

"My perfect match would be someone who likes to have fun, likes to stay active and busy, enjoys life, and is easy-going. I want to find my best friend and spend the rest of my life with her." *(Ah, isn't that romantic? I had read somewhere that women really respond to the idea of finding their best friend. Now that I'm married, I realize that the concept is true for both parties.)*

"I'm not a total health freak by any means but spend a lot of time keeping active. I love all kinds of exercise, especially walking, hiking, biking, jogging, strength-training, step aerobics and weightlifting. I work out in a gym a couple days every week and the rest of the time I exercise outdoors, which is my preferred location. When I travel, I pick activities that involve high levels of activity. I still enjoy spending quiet times walking in the woods or along a beach, though." *(At this point, if a woman didn't have access to pictures, they would probably think I looked like Tarzan. Looking back on this now, I realize that I really was a health freak. I wish I could find my freakiness again!)*

"My educational background is in music and secondary education. My major instrument was piano, and I minored in voice. I enjoy popular music of all kinds though, too, including country, rock, pop, folk – just about anything, so long as it has some kind of tonal center." *(I'm a music nerd. That means I pay nearly no attention whatsoever to popular music. Give me Beethoven any day. This seemed like a good compromise. At this point in my life, I hadn't finished my college degree either, a major ding against me, and I downplayed that demerit. See? Marketing. I'm happy to report that I did finish and earned my bachelor's degree shortly after getting married in 2012.)*

"My second educational journey was in secondary education. I majored in English and History. I'm also a history and political science buff, and I enjoy visiting and traveling to historical places and museums." *(Women love guys who are into museums, or so I've been told. With me, though, it's definitely true. I love to travel, and I love museums.)*

"I eat healthy ninety-five percent of the time. I enjoy eating out and trying new restaurants, and I don't mind eating unhealthy food once in a while. However, it's important to me that a match has a commitment to an overall healthy lifestyle, also. I battled weight issues for my entire life, and recently lost more than two hundred pounds without surgery. That's why a healthy lifestyle is so important to me now. I've been featured on *The Today Show* and *The 700 Club* to share my weight loss journey with others who struggle with their weight." *(Shameless self-promotion here. I thought some women would be intrigued by the idea of a guy who works hard enough to lose two hundred pounds WITHOUT surgery or by the idea of a guy who has been on national TV, and therefore must be famous. My goal here was mostly to try to intrigue women using the best cards I thought I had in my deck.)*

"I've always been described as a kind of "brainiac." I like trivia, read a lot, pay attention to current events, and stay on top of political stuff. I guess that makes me a bit of a nerd, but hey, nerds make great lovers, too." *(Aren't I cute? Wouldn't you be frantically moving your mouse to wink at me? I changed this part of my profile numerous times, finally deciding to play the "nerd" card which seemed to be growing in popularity.)*

What can I say? I was so clueless about the female gender in so many areas and probably still am! My wife told me the baseball photo caught her attention because she likes guys with facial hair. I chose to post it mainly to show that I do enjoy a traditional male activity and that I don't spend all my time with my nose buried in a book or sitting at the piano. I'm just glad it worked!

Janet winked at me first. I was shocked. Very few women had winked at me first. The fact that she winked first was huge.

I checked out Janet's profile and liked what I saw. Clearly, she was a very smart woman. Janet's profile was well-written and interesting. She was a scientist, and I knew that most scientists are very smart people. What I saw was a beautiful woman with a brain. I'm a sucker for smart women. My heart races at the thought of interesting conversations and a shared joy of kicking each other's butt in Scrabble!

I winked back, and so it began. We conversed for a period of time via the Match.com system. Janet told me about her education, her career, and other tidbits about her life. I did the same, being sure to embellish just enough to make myself sound like the Adonis I wanted her to think that I was.

Janet told me later that she was impressed with my wordiness and my writing skills. She was attracted to nerds, and I was definitely qualified. She also longed for interesting conversations, and I guess I am a rare find on the planet as a man who actually likes to have meaningful conversations about things other than sports.

At the height of our online conversations, we were discussing some social issues, and I got on my soap box. I fired off a ten-page email (not sure of the exact length now, but it was really long) and heard nothing for a day or two. I panicked. Had I gone too far? Was the issue we were discussing so important to her that if we disagreed the relationship was over?

A couple days later, the response came. "Wow, I am overwhelmed by the volume of your email. Why don't we get together and talk in person?"

SUCCESS! My wordiness opened the door to meet in person. Second base was clearly in view.

We made plans to meet at a local bookstore coffee shop. I was excited and nervous. In terms of dating skills, I was a 33-year-old high schooler. For more than a decade, I had intentionally avoided pursuing a relationship. Believing no woman would want the Pillsbury Doughboy, I had basically shut down my romantic inclinations and resigned myself to a life of singleness.

28

Now, after shedding a significant part of the Dough but still being very much a Boy, I wanted a woman! I read articles and advice columns from Match.com, eHarmony, Dr. Phil, Dr. Ruth, pretty much anyone I thought would have answers for what I should and should not do on a date. In the end, I resorted to just being myself.

An interesting thing happened on the way to that day at the bookstore. The evening before, my dad and I went to the local minor league baseball game. We both enjoy baseball and dad, who had grown up watching the Red Sox at Fenway Park, was a treasure trove of baseball trivia. After games, we would often stop at a local coffee shop.

As fate would have it, the coffee shop was near the bookstore where Janet and I were to meet. It was also very close to where she lived, although I didn't know that at the time. Dad and I entered the shop and headed to the counter. As we sat down, I glanced across the room, and was surprised to see a woman who looked very much like Janet.

At this point, I had not met her in person, so I was basing my analysis on pictures. I looked at her. She looked at me. I squinted and looked for recognizable features. She looked at me. I said to my dad, "I think that may be the woman I'm meeting for coffee tomorrow." My dad, in his typically unsubtle fashion, blurted out, "WHERE? WHERE?" and craned his neck to try and spot the woman to whom I was referring.

After a few minutes of squinting, craning, whispering and blurting, Janet walked over and said, "I think I'm supposed to meet you for coffee tomorrow."

The ice broke, and I beamed widely and said, "Yes. I wondered if you were Janet."

My dad was like a kid in the candy shop as he pumped Janet's hand vigorously. She excused herself and walked over to sit down with the OTHER guy she was meeting for coffee. She had more than one prospect, and there was my competition right across the room.

To be honest, I was also seeing another person at the time. We had met on eHarmony. She lived in Saginaw, which was about forty miles from where I lived, so I was apparently destined for long-distance relationships.

My dad was nearly uncontrollable at this point. I thought it was a very interesting coincidence that Janet and I had accidentally met the day before we were supposed to meet. My dad, who believes there is almost never anything that qualifies as a coincidence, immediately began telling me that God was at work and the Holy Spirit had directed this encounter.

"Take note, Jon, take note," he said. "God is speaking, God is moving, God is acting on your behalf."

Dad also knew that I was seeing another woman, and he also saw that Janet was seeing another man. My dad does have incredible spiritual intuition, although sometimes zeal gets mixed up in his intuition. At any rate, I smiled, and said something along the lines of, "We'll see how it goes."

At that moment, I was more interested in summing up my competition. It was not going in my favor, at least based on my incredibly warped analysis. Dude was tall, had no leftover flab, lacked man boobs, and was pretty smartly dressed. It looked like they were engaged in some pretty deep conversation.

I seriously considered walking over as I left and saying something like, "It was great to meet you in person. I'll see you tomorrow." Thankfully, common sense kicked in, because knowing my wife as I do now, that probably would have sunk all my chances with her.

I had to leave the coffee shop fairly quickly to get to another commitment. My dad wasn't in as much of a rush. I thought about telling him not to do anything crazy, but I figured he knew me well enough to not embarrass me. I have no idea why I thought that. I gave my dad a hug and said good night. I found out that he did indeed talk with Janet again, and said something along the lines of "God is at work" or some other spiritualization of the coincidence. I was embarrassed, but thankfully, Janet didn't hold it against me.

The next day, I headed back to Lansing. It was a beautiful, sunny morning, and I was excited. I must confess, the thought was running in the back of my mind that maybe, just maybe, God was on my side for once, and had orchestrated the unusual coincidence the evening before. Please don't misunderstand me; I do believe that God works on our behalf in numerous ways, seen and unseen. I'm just not convinced that direct divine intervention is a common, everyday occurrence.

Realizing that my competition had style, I had dressed smartly, or as smartly as I could while being completely dumb about fashion. I walked in, carrying myself with as much confidence as I could muster, and sat down at the table.

Don't worry; I'm not going to go into all the mushy gushy details. This isn't a romance novel, and even though I freely admit (to some people) that I am a romantic guy, you don't want to hear all the internal thoughts that were racing through my head.

Here's a brief summary: Janet had a beautiful voice. I could hear music in it, and being a musician, that was important to me. She was smart, unbelievably smart (and smarter than me), but I

31

was able to hold my own through most of our conversation. Janet was spiritual. I had prayed for a God-chaser; someone who, like me, pursued God with gusto, despite all the questions that seem to never have any answers. She loved nature, she loved music, including some of the same groups that I liked.

Probably ten minutes into this first date, I was feeling smitten. I liked her smile and could not get over her voice. It was like listening to opera every time she opened her mouth. She was smart and could have intelligent conversations. Interested and intrigued by the challenge of discussing new ideas and things I knew little about, such as plant genetics, her area of expertise, I decided to try to get the ball rolling.

"My brother and I were talking the other day about how the apples in the grocery stores are now the size of a baby's head," I said. "He told me he read something somewhere that said so many genetic modifications have been made to apples that they're no longer actually an apple," I said, with the utmost sincerity.

Janet stared at me for an uncomfortable amount of time. Uh oh. Had I said something offensive to a geneticist without even knowing it?

Suddenly, she smiled, and simply said "I think it's probably still an apple."

After we got to know each other much better and she learned of my family's tendency to speak in hyperbole or somehow latch on to the most abstract facts, we laughed about that moment. I'm so glad she didn't write me off for such an ignorant statement!

I wanted to get together with her again. So, I hatched a plan to convince her to give me another shot. What happened next may have sealed the deal, though, before I had a chance to implement my plan.

We approached the counter to pay for a book she was purchasing, and as we stood there, she reached down, pulled her cell phone off her belt clip, flipped it open, and said with confidence, "So, when can we get together again?"

Let me tell you folks, her confidence was incredibly sexy. I dislike weak and snively women. Janet oozed confidence. I probably sounded overly enthusiastic as I blurted out, "I'd love to do that; let me check my calendar!" and grabbed my cell phone.

We had identical phones. Another sign. One date led to another, and to another. Within two months, I had decided to end my other relationship (which wasn't going well anyhow) and focus my attention on Janet.

I could go on and on in great detail about our first year together. I remember nearly everything, because every moment was so monumental in my life. Janet's smarts and confidence continued to intrigue me more and more. For the first time, I fell hopelessly in love. As the saying goes, the rest is history, and after three years together, I decided I wanted to marry this amazing woman.

The day I proposed was a clear, cold day while visiting Chicago, and unfortunately, I was really sick. This was unusual, because in my new state of healthy living at the time, I hardly ever got sick. It was close to Christmas, and I had been tossing around the idea of proposing to Janet during the holidays. I even contacted a friend who had connections at the state capitol building in Lansing to see if it would be possible to get into the top of the Michigan capitol dome on Christmas Eve.

By this point, I knew Janet well enough to know that she has pretty strong opinions about things such as an engagement ring. Due to her line of work, Janet didn't wear much jewelry, so I was clueless as to what her preferences would be. I had been browsing jewelry stores and diligently setting aside money to purchase a ring. I knew that I couldn't afford the $10,000 model, and I knew that Janet wouldn't want a $10,000 ring anyhow. I figured my best option was to float a question to see if she would offer me some clue as to the type of ring she would want.

On our first full day in Chicago, Janet and I headed out to wander through the Polish Christmas festival. When the timing seemed right, I said, "So, if you were to have a ring, what type of ring would you like?"

Her eyes lit up like wildfire. In typical Janet fashion, she grabbed me by the arm and said, "Well, let's go find out!"

We pushed and shoved (mostly Janet doing the pushing and shoving and dragging me along) our way through the crowd at the festival and started looking for jewelry shops. We found several, and at the original Marshall Field's store (now Macy's) in the heart of downtown, she found a ring that she liked.

At this point, I was desperately trying to figure out how to proceed. It was still a few weeks before Christmas, and I still had the capitol dome idea in my head. Obviously, my question about the ring had clearly indicated to Janet what I was thinking about.

We found a ring that she liked that I was able to afford. She looked at me with wild anticipation in her eyes. I looked at her with anticipation and a little bit of fear What if she said no? She wanted that ring, and it was unique to that store because it was an heirloom ring. I took her aside, and said something like, "You like that ring a lot. Should I get that one?"

HOW INCREDIBLY LAME! Janet was practically trembling at this point. I had a whole mix of crazy thoughts and emotions going on because this was not how I had planned the process.

I realized I was being ridiculous. There was virtually no chance that we would be able to get into the capitol dome on Christmas Eve. I clearly loved her and wanted to marry her. Based on her reaction, I was pretty sure she was going to say yes. I bought the ring, but I REFUSED to officially propose inside of a Macy's store!

I immediately thought about the magic bean-shaped sculpture known as "Cloud Gate" in nearby Millennium Park. It was a spot we enjoyed every time we came to Chicago. I said, "I'll get the ring, and let's head over to the bean."

So, that's what we did. We walked over to the bean, I proposed, she said yes, and I started shouting, "I'M GETTING MARRIED!!" Many of the strangers checking out the bean cheered and congratulated us.

We asked some folks to take our picture. One of those pictures ended up on the cover of a magazine that profiled my weight loss story, which was really cool because it captures forever the love and excitement that we felt that day.

Janet and I were married in May 2012 at a beautiful country church nestled in patch of woods near Williamston, Michigan. My musical nerdiness meant I wanted a church with a pipe organ. We also needed more space than what was available in the church where my dad was a pastor. We invited about two hundred guests and fretted that with Michigan's unpredictable weather, we might end up with a cold and gloomy day – common for May in Michigan.

What we got instead was a heat wave! It was ninety-four degrees that day, and our beautiful church had no air conditioning. We and our guests sweated it out during a lovely ceremony Janet and I planned together that included a lot of singing. Janet was radiantly beautiful in her gown and came down the aisle as the organist let loose with the beautiful Beethoven-inspired hymn, "Joyful, Joyful, We Adore Thee." I was so excited I didn't even notice the heat.

Afterwards, we met our guests at a reception at a local golf course. It was wonderful to see so many people who meant so much to both of us. We spent our first night as a married couple at a local bed and breakfast and then spent the next day relaxing and exploring Williamston.

Then, Janet prepared to return to our new home in Nebraska, while I picked up a moving truck and loaded up my belongings for the long trek west to join her.

Our new life together began on the Great Plains of the U.S. in a new city where we knew no one but would soon fall in the love with the warmth, diversity and vibrancy of Lincoln, Nebraska, our home for the next five years. Nebraska is so much more than corn, with friendly people who embraced us with warmth and hospitality. It was a wonderful place to start our new life together.

4

Carland

Carland may sound like a bad place to buy a used car, but in reality, it's my hometown. A former stop on the Ann Arbor railroad, Carland had its heyday in the early part of the twentieth century and at one time, had a school, gas station, general store, barbershop, post office, and large grain elevator.

Most of these buildings are still standing, many with their false fronts and appearing like they were stolen from the set of Little House on the Prairie. My family lived one mile east of Carland when I was born, and the town had started to decline. When my family returned to Carland in the early 1990s, the only business left was the grain elevator.

These days, Carland's population has dwindled to one hundred or so residents. The entire town consists of a row of houses and former businesses on both sides of the aptly named Carland Road. While the road itself extends several miles, the town itself occupies a stretch of only about a quarter mile.

As I mentioned previously, I lived near Carland at two different points in time. For obvious reasons, I don't remember much from the first stint, since I was only zero to three years old! Most of my Carland stories and experiences occurred after we returned in 1991, just prior to my sophomore year in high school.

If you were born and raised in Carland, there's a good chance that you are or were a McNeth, married a McNeth, were related to a McNeth, and saw or interacted with a McNeth daily. The McNeth family were some of Carland's original settlers. The family's second generation consisted of ten children. Another branch of the family was also widely dispersed in the area, although not in Carland itself.

Our church consisted of many McNeth's. My closest friends were McNeth's. I was an honorary McNeth. Carland could have just as easily been named McNethville.

My friend Jared, a frequent character in other chapters, was born and lived in Carland, and you guessed it – he was a McNeth. Jared enjoyed antiques and collectibles and had a small shop at the back of his parent's property where he kept many of his treasures. We would hang out back there and discuss world politics and other things that guys who are into antiques enjoy discussing.

There was always a well-stocked supply of Little Debbie snack cakes, donuts and diet soda on hand. Jared's family, along with our friends from north of town, Raylene and Brandy, constituted our local gang – the Carland Hounds. Most of us also had weight issues, so being fat or talking about our "pork," as we liked to call it, was a frequent activity.

Jared had a special name and story for nearly every inhabitant of Carland, or at least the ones near his house. There was "Fudge and Cleo," the elderly couple across the street; "Jiffy-Huat Baking Mix," the outcast teenager next door to Fudge and Cleo; "Kkkaattiee Koomma," the nosy neighbor farther down the street, and the list goes on and on.

Jared also had a gaggle of cats of dubious quality. His family called them, "kitas," a slang term of Czech origin, as his family on his mother's side was of Czech descent. Sometimes, due to the volume of kitas, it was necessary to use only identifying characteristics as part of the naming process.

During my high school years, the McNeth kita brood consisted of "Night of the Living Dead Kita," so named for her miraculous ability to survive multiple episodes of being run over in the road; "The Bitcher," the cranky tomcat responsible for most of the rest of the gaggle's existence; "Puffy Kita," with the requisite longhair coat; "Mrs. Mumumra," the cat who looked like it had stepped off the set of The Adaams Family; "Black Kita" and "White Kita," I'm assuming you have the cognitive ability to figure out the origin of those names; and "Funkarella," the kita with an unfortunate mixture of unusual colors and birth defects resulting in a face that looked like it had been slammed into the wall several times.

In addition to their cats, the McNeth's had an interesting array of vehicles. Their dad worked for one of the Big Three automakers in Flint, and due to the family's size, they generally owned the required boat-like cars to accommodate them. This was also very important because the McNeth's descended from giants, and most of them were over six feet tall – both male and female.

Jared's sister and my girlfriend, Kristie, was the oldest in their family and needed a car to commute to Michigan State University where she was a student. Her dad purchased a 1979 Oldsmobile Delta 98 for the family, but in reality, it was mostly Kristie's car to get to school. It quickly became our shuttle.

We went everywhere in that car. It was a true, throwback cruiser, and we actually did cruise in it in the cruising loop in downtown Owosso, near where we lived. Kristie drove while we cruised because it took a lot of paying attention to keep the loop moving, and the rest of us were distracted with our fifty-nine cent tacos from Taco Bell.

Things were going well for the Oldsmobile until one night when Kristie, her sister Daphne, Jared, and I were coming home late from cruising in Owosso. We headed down the darkened Carland Road. Suddenly…WHAM!!! The windshield cracked in a thousand directions and the headlights went out.

"I think I hit something!!!" screamed Kristie.

The rest of us looked at each other, a bit perplexed, but chocked up the statement to shock at what had just happened.

"I think it was a deer," I said.

"But I didn't see a deer," Kristie said.

"Neither did I, but I see a smashed-up windshield and tufts of light brown hair stuck in the windshield wipers, so I'm pretty sure it was a deer," I said.

Daylight confirmed I was correct. It was to be the first of at least a dozen car-deer encounters I survived over the course of the years living in Carland. The beasts were simply everywhere in the many surrounding wooded areas. My mom hit two within the course of about three months. We locals learned the importance of high-beam headlights, driving slowly at night, and low-deductible comprehensive insurance coverage.

Kristie continued to drive the banged-up Oldsmobile for several more months. It was never quite the same, though. The ride wasn't as smooth, it took quite a bit of work to get the front doors open and closed, and the windshield looked like a jigsaw puzzle.

Once, in a particularly reflective moment of trying to see through the puzzle, Kristie turned to me and said, "I've been examining my crack, and I noticed that it's spreading."

I blinked a few times while my mind processed what I had just heard and then burst into laughter. To this day, we have never let her live down that illustrious statement!

As if hitting a deer weren't bad enough, another of my friends had the misfortune of hitting a horse on Carland Road. The poor animal had apparently wandered out of the barn at a home that was notorious for sundry loose animals wandering all over the place, although it was far more likely you would encounter a goose in the road and not Mr. Ed.

Somehow, the horse survived. The car had a large hoofprint in the back panel where the ticked off animal apparently kicked the car after it stopped. While hitting animals of many persuasions was a rather common occurrence among the inhabitants of Carland, I think my friend may have the honor of being the only resident to hit a horse.

Another of the endearing things about Carland was the local Carland Cable Network (CCN). The network consisted of phone lines, originally part of the Ma Bell system, eventually sold to General Telephone (GTE) and then sold to Verizon and finally to Frontier, whose goal is to completely neglect them. An important part of the network, however, consisted of the Carland Grandmas. The Grandmas kept everyone else informed of what was going on in Carland, both true and false, via the aforementioned phone lines.

One could usually spot the Network in action when walking or driving through Carland and seeing a Grandma at the window with the curtain pulled back slightly to one side and the phone against her ear. The Grandmas of the CCN were assisted greatly by the existence of a party line system until well into the 1980s.

For those who may not know, party lines were the norm in many rural areas for much longer than most places. Two or more houses shared the same phone line and number. A light on the rotary dial phone was supposed to glow when a "party" other than yourself was using the phone. Many of these lights were conveniently burned out, however.

Of course, you would know immediately if someone else was using the phone, because upon picking it up, you would hear the conversation. Most of the time, if this occurred, you would simply gently return the phone to the cradle and try again later. However, the Grandmas knew how to maximize time on inadvertent phone pick-ups to acquire details to be passed along to other Grandmas on the network.

These bits of information often morphed into misinformation, resulting in some pretty hilarious rumors at times. It was all part of small-town life, and generally, the rumors were innocuous enough that no harm was caused.

However, I do recall my dad having a difficult conversation with the person who shared our line because she would listen in on some of his conversations with parishioners, which often included personal details. Thankfully, by the time we returned to Carland, party lines had gone the way of the dodo bird.

Carland had its fair share of characters, including the members of my own family, but one particularly interesting individual comes to mind. Daisy had been born and raised in Carland and remained nearby after marrying. Her son, Tony, was in our local 4-H Club, until he was banned by the County Extension for cheating on his county fair entries.

4-H, in and of itself, was an interesting experience. When most people hear 4-H, they think of animals. Indeed, the county fairgrounds had large barns built for the purpose of exhibiting any number of farm animals and household pets. Our club, consisting mostly of members from the metropolis of Carland, lacked many entries for animals.

We did have a few local farm kids that participated, but most of us entered things like food creations, writing samples, sewing, and plants or vegetables. I must brag for a moment and tell you I am the proud recipient of two Superior and Best in Class ribbons from the fair – one for my family's historical peach pie recipe, and the other for a satirical writing sample I wrote as part of a school assignment.

4-H meetings were also an opportunity to eat lots of yummy food, something I and many other of the club members really enjoyed. My award-winning peach pie was enjoyed by everyone during the "sample" phase prior to entry, and I eagerly gobbled down Jared's Czech pastry creations. Food was nearly always at the forefront of my mind, and it was evident in how I greedily consumed the snacks and samples during our meetings.

Back to Daisy and her son...they participated in our club on and off, but Tony never seemed to be very engaged. He was more of a motorhead than a farmer or baker. Daisy usually pressured him into entering something, so we were all a bit surprised to see him turn in a form to submit a decorated cake and a floral arrangement. While the 4-H rules allowed for guidance from adults for items being entered in the fair, the actual entry was supposed to be created only by the entrant. And we all were dubious about Tony's cake decorating and floral arrangement skills.

On the day for taking entries to the show barn, Jared was on a mission to see what Tony actually entered. We dropped off our items to be judged and then headed into the show barn to see if his items had been put out yet for display. Usually, items were processed when you brought them to the show barn and then put out for the public to view. At some point during the week of the fair, a panel of esteemed judges would walk through the show barn and judge the entries.

Jared spotted the cakes. His sister, Daphne, was the expert cake decorator in our club. In fact, she went on to have a successful cake decorating business and did the cake for my wedding. I think Jared was partly motivated to find out what Tony was up to because of loyalty to Daphne and a general dislike for Daisy. We made a beeline for the cakes.

Tony's cake sat near the middle of the group. It was beautiful. Big, colorful flowers with expertly created petals, lovely cursive writing and a section that looked like a small garden adorned the top of the snow-white base frosting.

"There's no way he did this," said Jared.

"I can't believe Daisy could pull off something this nice either," I said.

Suspicious, we began to hunt for the floral arrangements. Spotting them a few rows over, we crept over and began examining the entry tags. We found Tony's stunning arrangement. It stood out from most of the others due to its creative color profile, complexity, and professional appearance.

Jared was now in full investigative mode. Looking around gingerly to see if anyone was watching, he picked up the arrangement. Much to his chagrin, or perhaps delight, he could clearly see the remains of a sticker with a local grocery store's logo on the bottom of the vase holding the arrangement. Jared suspected cake and floral treachery.

However, it was going to take more than just that sticker to prove anything was untoward. Entrants could purchase vases and flowers from various places; they just had to do the arranging themselves. Jared was convinced that Tony's arrangement was a pre-made one from the store's floral department, though. He also suspected the same store had done the cake decorating.

"Let's go," he said.

We made our way back to the car and high-tailed it to the grocery store. This was in the days before cell phones and their cameras existed, but luckily for Jared, he had his primitive by today's standards digital camera in the car as he used it to photograph antiques for sale. We entered the store and headed first to the floral section.

Sure enough, right there in front, on prominent display, was Tony's arrangement. Jared had a hard time containing his glee as he snapped several photos.

We then headed over to the cakes. I suspected this one might be more difficult to prove because if Tony's cake had been ordered as a unique creation, there would be no evidence. As fate or luck would have it, Tony, his mom, or both had picked up a pre-made design and simply had the bakery put the writing on it. In the cake cooler sat two more cakes with the same design, minus the words.

"Wow," I said.

"We gotta tell the cops," said Jared.

"How about we just tell the people in charge at the fair?" I suggested.

And so we did. After an investigation and interview, Daisy and Tony were banned from ever again entering items in the County Fair. I don't recall what reasons or excuses they gave, but it is certainly something that went down in the lore of the Carland Variety 4-H Club, which disbanded a few years later upon most of the club graduating from high school.

Later that same year, I was on my way home from the pizza shop where I worked. I drove by Daisy and Tony's house and noticed they had put up their Christmas decorations. They generally had a nice display, so I slowed a bit to take it all in.

Lights were blinking, a light up snowperson or two was in the yard, and then I saw stretched across the front of the house something written in lights wrapped in greenery.

"JEASUS IS THE REASON" the lights said.

I did a doubletake.

"JEASUS IS THE REASON" the lights continued to blink.

I was gobsmacked. Tempted to pull in the driveway and knock on the door, I thought better of it due to my general anxiety about confrontation and knocking on doors in a community where both cows and guns outnumber people.

I arrived home shortly thereafter and told my parents what I had seen. My mom refused to believe it. I told her I had verified it several times. My sister, who was visiting from Ohio that weekend, was laughing hysterically. Although she knew who Daisy was, she didn't know any of the details of our interactions related to cake and floral treachery. She opened the drawer and found Daisy's phone number.

We all waited on bated breath.

"Hello? Is this Daisy? Hi Daisy, this is one of your neighbors. Did you know that you have Jesus' name spelled incorrectly in the display in front of your house?"

There was momentary silence on the other end. Then we all heard a loud, "What??"

"Yeah, you have Jesus' name spelled wrong. There is no "A" in Jesus," my sister said.

Daisy suddenly responded very loudly, "Tony, you dummy, you spelled Jesus' name wrong!!!"

We could hear some muffled protests from Tony in the background. Daisy abruptly hung up.

I grabbed the phone from my sister and hurriedly called Jared to relay the story. He was laughing hysterically and kept trying out different pronunciations of "JEASUS."

"Gee-AH-soos," he said. "No, wait. "Gia-soos."

I interrupted him.

"Clearly it's "Gee-ay-sus," I said. "There's a Gee-ay-sus sign in Daisy's tree," I laughed, thinking of the first day of Christmas from the classic song.

And that folks, is how the Carland Hounds came to write our own Carland version of "The Twelve Days of Christmas" for the next ten or so years, but always ending in resounding joy with "And a Gee-ay-sus sign in Daisy's tree!"

As a humorist, it's easy for me to recall the hilarity of high school follies, the eccentric neighbors and characters who lived there, and many other laughable experiences. But Carland was also a town of loving, caring people who looked out for each other. If someone was ill, or if their house burned down, Carlandites quickly mounted a support network to help. It is the quintessential small-town America that many people talk about and recall with fondness, and I am blessed to call it my hometown.

5

Donuts

I'm not quite sure when I first fell in love with donuts. I am specifically attracted to cream-filled long-johns or "crème sticks," depending on what part of the country you're from. I've rarely met a donut I didn't feel like consuming. In fact, I've rarely met a donut that I didn't end up consuming, except during years when I was on the donut wagon and denied myself the joy of donut-eating altogether.

The beauty of the crème-filled donut is lost on many individuals, so let me explain my infatuation. Not only is its outside gloriously plump and glistening with the chosen variety of grease and frosting, but the inside is a conclave of love. Yes, hidden within this log of love is a deliciously sweet and succulent center...the crème zone.

The crème zone is like heaven has come down to earth, for one brief moment, and the pastry gods have selected you as the chosen one. The zone, in all its addictive glory, is a place where many a man, including me, have thrown common sense and nutrition facts out the window in pursuit of the thrill of donut-y decadence.

A bit of personal pastry history is perhaps helpful in understanding my donut addiction. I first recall encountering donuts at a young age within the confines of my own mother's kitchen. A hearty woman of German stock, my mother would periodically fry up her own homemade donuts in the electric skillet. Although these dull, brown lumps would soon be cast aside for more voluptuous choices, I loved those donuts. I couldn't get enough of those doughy, fried lumps, and even earned a spanking when mom discovered that I had eaten an entire batch.

In elementary school, I was exposed to Mister Donut, the local donut chain where we lived in Canton, Ohio. Oh yes, there were other donut shops, but Mister Donut had it all. The donuts were prepared on site, and you could watch the miraculous process through a viewing window. Each carefully hand-crafted masterpiece lovingly made its way through a vat of pig grease to a conveyer belt where workers would caress and massage the finished creation into the true object of my desires – the crème stick, their chosen name for a crème-filled donut.

My father and I spent many happy hours in the booth at the Mister Donut crack house. My dad is a studious guy who also enjoys donuts. Like most addictions, there is probably a genetic predisposition at play in donut obsession. Dad and I usually began with two crème sticks each. Dad would get coffee, and I would get a diet soda. Fat people drink a lot of diet soda especially with fast food or "fast" donuts. It doesn't make sense, but it makes us feel better about the thousands of other calories we are consuming at the same time.

Dad would slowly drink his coffee, eat his donuts, and read his Bible. Did you know eating donuts is a religious experience? Sugar-induced religious euphoria is one of the acceptable euphorias for Christians, and one that many experience every Sunday as they wander through the pre-worship fellowship and load up on sugar and caffeine before entering an atmosphere of peaceful worship. Go figure. Oops, a rabbit trail...sorry. Follow me back to dad and Mister Donut.

I spent a lot of time with my dad in situations like these. Dad liked to read his Bible and study...in a restaurant. Mom liked me to be out of her hair. I knew that dad was relatively clueless about what I ate and would be more likely to allow me to indulge my donut fantasy. So, we spent many hours out of the house together.

Dad would enter his spiritual zone, and I would usually read a book or the newspaper. My two introductory donuts quickly gave way to three and then four, and then if dad really wasn't paying attention, maybe five or six or more.

I was quickly becoming a donut junkie. One was never enough; a minimum of six were required to obtain the same high. I was turning into a donut addict. Reinforcing this addiction was the fact that much of the positive time spent with my dad centered around eating donuts or food at other restaurants. Both made me happy and often occurred simultaneously.

My donut addiction continued to blossom, and by the time I was in high school, I was strung out. I was eating upwards of a dozen donuts every week, usually in secret. Just like any other addiction, I committed my sin under wraps.

I would occasionally allow myself to be seen indulging, but would usually only publicly eat one donut, and then stash extras in my pockets, my car, or the inside of my coat. It's altogether possible I may have shoved a couple of crème sticks down my pants. I don't recall doing it, but in the midst of the addictive fog, it could have happened.

I also found a donut-buddy. Jared struggled with his weight, too, although he wore his weight better. He was fortunate to be more than six feet tall, which helped stretch him out a bit. I never made it past five nine, which meant I looked like a life-size jelly donut myself.

Jared introduced me to the local dealer, White's Bakery. By this time in my life, the small stuff no longer had the intended effect. I had moved past gateway donuts to the big guns. White's was my crack house. Jared and I were regular junkies showing up on its doorstep. Occasionally, we would meet other donut-heads while there, but we always hoped to beat them to the really good stuff.

Jared and I would usually head to White's on Saturday while we were in town for other legitimate activities. Fortunately, White's was a bit off the beaten path, and most recreational users were long-gone by the time we arrived. If we were lucky, we might get our fix on clearance pastries.

Jared wasn't as particular about his variety as I was. He not only celebrated donut diversity, he was willing to engage with any and all varieties. That was fine with me, because I had developed a somewhat exclusive attitude about my donuts; I only wanted the crème-filled long johns.

We cleared White's out. I'm not exaggerating. We would leave with perhaps two or three dozen donuts between the two of us. Often, I'd be jamming my donut into my mouth before we even made it out of the store. Jared had more self-control, but I could see the sweat forming on his forehead if transactions took too long. I had the shakes as soon as the bag was in my hand. It was pleasant relief to grab that first donut and feel the euphoric rush.

White's was aware of the shame of donut addiction, so the counter girl usually gave us one large bag so we could put our many smaller bags inside. This helped us avoid being seen walking out of the store with ten bags of donuts. We would jump in the car, and usually head down to a parking lot by the river. It wasn't a van (fans of Chris Farley and SNL will get that line), but although we didn't realize or acknowledge it at the time, we were definitely limiting our future prospects in life because we were donut junkies.

"Oh my God, this is the best donut ever," Jared would say as he rustled through his pile, which usually included iced cookies and crème horns.

A crème horn is a distantly related cousin of the crème stick and crème-filled long john. Instead of the outside "dough" of the donut, a crème horn had a hard, pastry shell coated in sugar. The center was filled with a crème of slightly different taste and texture than a crème-filled donut. Kind of like some other recreational drugs – slightly different taste and texture, but the same effect. Jared loved crème horns, probably more than crème sticks. And he also loved kolaches and badges – two Czech pastries. I loved them too. In fact, I never met a Czech pastry I didn't crave.

"No way," I said. "This crème stick (I still had a hard time remembering to call them long johns in Michigan) is delicious. And so is this one, and this one, and oh my God, did you find badges? Can I have some? I'll trade you two cream cheese donuts and an apple fritter for six of your badges."

And so it went. We sat there stuffing our faces until both of us started belching and seeing double as our blood sugar steadily rose. We would eventually pass out and sit by the river, strung out, until our blood sugar returned to safe levels and our vision was restored. Nine times out of ten, we'd return home with evidence of our binger in the form of sprinkles on our collar or a telltale oily blob on our shirt where crème had shot out of the end of the long john before we had a chance to prevent it. Powdered sugar everywhere was further evidence of our sin.

53

Long-term donut addiction can lead to heart attacks and strokes. Donut addicts usually morph into looking like the object of their affections. Beside the fact that donuts are addictive and taste like heaven, just what is it that makes them so appealing?

Nothing.

When you really stop and think about it, there is absolutely nothing that is realistically appealing about a donut. It's a squamous mass of fatty dough, sometimes so squamous and fatty that you can actually squeeze grease out of it, filled with a chemically nebulous gelatinous or crème-like material with some frosting on top.

YUCK! I won't even go into the nutrition facts. Suffice it to say, if you use a daily calorie tracker, you can quit after breakfast if you eat a donut.

Donuts and crack are remarkably similar because of what happens in the brain when you eat or snort. Being fat doesn't have much to do with your stomach; it's more about your head and the brain inside of it. If you want to peg blame on some body part for your weight issues, that's the best place to start. I have another chapter devoted to that, so for now, you'll have to take me at my word.

Jared and I have both been on and off the donut wagon repeatedly in life. These days, I'm glad to once again be happily riding on the wagon. But it's a lifelong struggle and one that will never go away. Like most addictions, I have several steps to keep me securely in my seat on the wagon. The most effective one is reminding myself I want to stay alive and enjoy life past age sixty.

That's a powerful motivator. Nothing tastes as good as being alive is a phrase I would tell myself often. Sometimes it's necessary to really confront yourself with the truth, and I had to admit that as much as I love them, donuts cannot be part of my life – ever.

6

I'm German – I'll Eat Anything with Sausage, Noodles, or Type 2 Diabetes

I love my family. We are quirky and have moments when we fight like redneck clans on *Cops*, but we have always managed to forgive, mostly forget, and move on. I hesitated to write anything about my family, but then realized that my weight problem has ties to my family and my family has weight problems. So, I guess I'll start by just running down through the list.

Welcome to the Stanton clan. Hold on tight, because we Stanton's are known for wild rides. We are unabashedly loud, fiercely loyal (usually), zany, and almost always a guaranteed fun time. Just ask anyone who knows us well.

My parents are your classic case of opposites attract. My mom was raised on a farm in a household of German origin where women were meant to be quiet and the cows out in the field were louder than the conversation around the dinner table. My dad was raised in Boston (can we say city boy?), and his family talked and fought furiously around the dinner table, usually about politics, and specifically about the Kennedys, a major topic of discussion in many Massachusetts homes during the 1960s. My parents' families were about as different as night and day.

Interestingly, both of my parents had weight problems growing up. My dad, with whom I share a lot of physical characteristics, was pudgy as a kid, stocky as a youth and had man boobs that were at least as big as mine if not bigger. He slimmed down some in college, and by the time he met my mom, he weighed about 170 pounds on a five eight frame. Not too shabby. I wish I could say that I was 170 pounds when I met my wife!

Dad seemed to always be on a diet during my growing up years. I remember him trying several diet fads and have watched him "ride the yo-yo" for essentially his entire life. So have I. Dad does his best. I do my best. Somewhere, in the helixes of DNA circulating through the Stanton body resides a sinister strand. It sucks. Everyone has their battles, but our battle is always on public display, and there's no pill to cure it. That's the way it goes sometimes.

I've often wondered why most Stantons have weight issues. My Stanton cousin, Sally, is a genealogist. She traced back the Stanton line and discovered that at least three of our ancestors survived the Mayflower expedition to the new world.

If you recall your high school history lessons, the people that survived the Mayflower likely had genetic predisposition to storing fat and using it slowly. Hence, they survived the famine of that first winter.

My cousin blames those genes for our Stanton portliness. We were on the Mayflower. We survived. It makes perfect sense, except we don't generally have to worry anymore about fighting someone for a moldy potato in the hold of a ship in order to eat. We just go to McDonald's. See the problem?

My mom is tall, especially for a woman. She takes after my grandmother, who was five eleven and had bones the size of baseball bats and hips the size of Vesuvius. My mom is a bit shorter (five nine) but has grandma's bone structure. She also worked extremely hard on the farm. My mom was the type you wouldn't want to meet in a dark alley. She says she was teased a lot, but I believe that if she had decided to take matters in her own hands, the bully would have been squashed.

By the time mom graduated from high school, she was pushing 280 pounds. A lot of it was muscle, but a fair amount was down-home German cooking. Dumplings and homemade noodles aren't exactly health food. However, by the time my mom met my dad and walked down the aisle, she was a trim 135 pounds.

During her first two years of college, mom decided to address her weight problem. It worked. More importantly, she learned

lifelong habits that have stuck with her. My mom has kept her weight at a healthy level for more than forty years!

My mom was really happy for me when I finally lost 230 pounds in 2009. We agreed that I must have inherited her willpower. To honor my mom after I lost my weight, we had this photo taken.

That's both of us inside my former pants! Mom laughed, (everyone laughed, of course) but I think I also saw a tear in her eye. Mom knew what it was like to be fat and to be picked on because of it. She was constantly worried about my weight, and as a result, she was often on my case about it. I know my mom's intentions were good, and came from a place of love and concern, but as a kid, I interpreted those concerns as "you're not good enough," and "no one is going to love and accept you unless you lose weight." I still struggle with those thoughts, especially when I've failed yet again and dove headfirst into a plate of schnitzel or eaten the entire pan of cinnamon rolls.

My oldest sister, Deb, is beautiful. Of the four of us with blue eyes, hers are the bluest and she is quite possibly one of the sweetest souls to grace the universe. Deb, like me, has battled weight her entire life. She also was heavy growing up and took a lot of razzing because of it.

By the time she was in high school, she had found a way to control her weight and was slim. Her hair probably contributed a quarter or more of her weight. It was the height of the big-hair 80s, so taking that into consideration, she was very slim. Deb, like so many of us, has been on the yo-yo ever since.

My sister, Becka, is also beautiful. Becka's beauty radiates from her joyful, funky spirit. Becka battled weight later in life. She was never thin and trim (in the way that our culture seems to demand anyhow) during her growing up years, but she wasn't as heavy as Deb and me.

Becka's battle, as is the case for many women, came after she began having kids. Becka also developed a food addiction as a mechanism for coping with a difficult life and dealing with past demons that haunted her. Food addiction is real, and it runs in my family. By the time Becka had her last child, she was pushing 320 pounds. She decided to have bariatric surgery and lost a lot of weight, although she has had some health struggles and challenges ever since.

Finally, there's my brother Dave. Dave inherited a different set of genes. While he's not overly tall, Dave doesn't have the stocky Stanton build. He takes more after my mom's side of the family, which did include a few tall and skinny folks, especially on my grandmother's side.

Dave's build was discussed often in our household and was usually shared with new people we met in our family's many moves. Dave clearly was skinny while the rest of us looked like tanks, and I guess we felt the need to explain. Frequently. It wasn't helpful to the rest of us to be reminded constantly that Dave was the skinny one. I know it caused me to continually feel inferior.

Dave has a great heart, and I don't think there's anyone that he won't help in whatever way he can. My brother and I had a difficult relationship growing up. Dave was athletic and good looking. I was un-athletic, fat, ugly, and a nerd. All brothers fight during their growing up years, and we were no exception. I definitely harbored some jealousy toward my brother, mostly because of his ability to eat whatever he wanted and stay perfectly thin.

In our adult years, we have maintained a good relationship even though we see the world somewhat differently. Dave's a free spirit. As an adult, he has started to have some weight issues. Although he is probably the most hyper person I know, I think his metabolism has begun the slow decline that inevitably comes as we age.

So, there you have it, my quirky family in a nutshell. You can certainly see a common theme: FAT. Every single one of us has dealt or is dealing with being overweight, and often with being extremely obese. Why is that? What's going on?

Believe me, if I had the answer and solution, I'd be writing a completely different book. Yes, genetics plays a role. Each member of my family is a walking poster child for genetics and weight issues. It's generational. It extends to our extended family. But it's not all about genetics. Genetics may result in a slower metabolism and make it more difficult to maintain a healthy weight, but it's not an issue that can't be overcome. My mom and I are perfect examples of that.

My family's weight problem has more to do with environment, I believe, than it does with anything genetic. You see, my family celebrates with food, and we celebrate in a big way! We really don't know how to not make holidays, and birthdays, and any family gathering all about food.

Our family also had some basic food rules during our growing up years. "Clean up your plate" and "don't waste food" were two big ones. While well-intentioned, we often pushed ourselves beyond "full" to meet these requirements, and that became a habit over time. Add in some denial, some psychological pain and distress, include the aforementioned genetics as a garnish, and you have the perfect cocktail for a significant weight problem.

Many families celebrate with food. America's holidays were born around the table and continue to be celebrated around the table. Food is part of our culture. That's not necessarily a bad thing, but it can become a bad thing when certain patterns develop. I didn't recognize the pattern of the Stanton celebrations until I met my wife's family.

My wife's family also celebrates with food. My mother-in-law is a wonderful cook. We all look forward to Thanksgiving, Christmas, and pretty much every other meal that she makes. The same is true with my mom. However, the two tables look very different.

Since we've been married, Janet and I have had dual holiday celebrations if we made the trip back to Michigan. Typically, we would have Thanksgiving/Christmas lunch with her family and dinner with my family. These were gut-busting days, although we made half-hearted attempts to prevent copious overeating.

At Janet's parents' home, the table is set immaculately and the cuisine and how it's served mirrors the best five-star establishments. We all gather around a rectangular table and Janet's father serves us the three or four traditionally prepared items. Dessert may or may not be served immediately afterwards. The portions fill the plate, but don't weigh it down. Seconds are rare. It took me a while to get used to meals with my in-laws because it was a completely foreign environment compared to my own family's way of eating together.

I'll never forget the first time Janet joined my family for a meal. There was so much noise in the room that in order to participate in one of the four simultaneous conversations, shouting was the only option. Hand gestures helped as well. Pictionary was available via your napkin if the din became completely overwhelming. Janet had a look of shock on her face, and we had just arrived.

My family gathers around a large round table. We often eat on paper plates because with no dishwasher, my mom doesn't want to spend two hours doing all the dishes afterwards. I don't blame her. She might be able to secure some help, but usually my family eats so much that everyone wants to lumber into the living room and crash until the sugar high wears off.

The center of the table is completely covered with ten to twelve different food items. Most of them are large, sweet, buttery, or otherwise artery-clogging, except for the veggie tray and maybe a salad.

Recall that my mom's roots are German, and that impacts her cooking and the cooking she has passed on to my siblings and me. We will eat anything that involves sausage, noodles, or Type 2 diabetes. Large slabs of meat (usually more than just one animal option available), biscuits, rolls, homemade noodles, candied sweet potatoes, sweet applesauce, homemade jams and jellies (minimum of four cups of sugar per batch), and the list goes on…and we haven't even made it to the desserts yet. Cakes, cookies, several varieties of pie, shortbread, cheesecake…do you feel stuffed yet?

Dinner usually begins with a prayer, and then a loud argument ensues about which way to pass the food. My nephew, impervious to the conversation, usually stands up, leans over whomever it's necessary to bypass, and grabs four biscuits. Eventually, someone wins the argument about which way to pass the food, and it's off to the races!

To truly be a Stanton, it's necessary to heap at least a thousand calories on your plate during the first go-around. Usually, there's not enough room on the plate for everything, so items that aren't wet get set to the side of the plate. For instance, my plate is usually surrounded with a biscuit, carrot sticks, and other items that won't soak into the tablecloth.

My sisters are usually talking to each other about their menstrual cycles, while mediating their children's desires to eat only biscuits or to steal food off each other's plates. It's not unusual for my brother to lob biscuits from one end of the table to the other. The food goes around so quickly that if anyone takes too long and creates a bottleneck, there will be words exchanged.

Everyone is fighting over who has the jelly, where's the ketchup, and what is wrong in Washington, DC. My family breaks every rule of decorum when it comes to eating together. We talk almost exclusively about religion, sex, money, politics, and bodily functions.

At Janet's first meal, I gave her tremendous credit because she made it through the first half-hour with her sanity intact. At some point, I looked over and saw that her face indicated an overwhelming desire to flee the premises. I had seen similar looks shortly before vomiting. I asked her if she would like to take a walk. She immediately said, "YES!" grabbed my hand and yanked me out the door.

Janet and I laugh (usually) now, because over time, we have both adjusted. We now realize that our families are our own version of the movie *My Big Fat Greek Wedding*. I have absolutely no doubt that my brother would roast an animal in the front yard if given the opportunity. My dad doesn't use Windex to cure everything, but instead relies on the Holy Spirit. Feeling bad? Job going poorly? Pain in your stomach? The Holy Spirit is the answer to everything and will resolve your woes.

The Stanton family's food culture is quite obviously a recipe for obesity. It's not intentional. It's not like my mom sits down and says to herself, "Gee, I wonder what I can make for Thanksgiving that will make everyone fatter." My sisters don't plan their contributions to the meal to result in self-loathing, frequent trips to the bathroom, and rampant flatulence. Over time, it's just become the nature of who we are. It's our food culture. We're used to it, and our taste buds are used to it, also.

As I think back, what's perhaps most significant about all of this is when Janet shared her perceptions of my family's food culture with me after that first meal, I was completely clueless. I had no idea what she was talking about. Well, that may be stretching it a bit, but it's very true that my family's normal was exceptionally abnormal to Janet and probably to many others as well. We were unaware that food was the central theme of our family gatherings. We simply did what we always had done.

In order to maintain this status quo, a bit of denial is necessary. Perhaps the greatest disconnect that existed in these meal scenarios is that every single one of us were facing significant challenges in our lives that were tied to weight. I am convinced that our ability to miss the connection between eating 3,000 calories while talking about how unhappy life is because of weight, or discussing the latest pill needed for a weight-related health issue, was rooted in a psychology of denial.

I suspect that my thoughts and feelings about myself were also how my other family members thought about themselves at times. They may not have been exactly the same, and our ways of thinking about and dealing with them may have been a bit different. However, for most of us, food was a comfort agent to help cope with the reality of how we felt about ourselves.

This, my friends, is how food addiction develops. Food addiction is insidious, not only because the method of soothing only makes the root problem worse, but also because you can't quit cold turkey. You have to eat cold turkey, or some other type of food, in order to survive. It's not like you can simply give up eating.

I'm not sure why food became the Stanton family coping agent of choice, but I think the food culture in which we lived made it a natural method. We feel bad about ourselves, and food makes us feel good.

In my family's world, taking drugs, drinking too much, gambling, or having sex with multiple partners is sinful. Sinners go to hell. We're already bad enough and fighting tooth and nail to stay out of hell. Surely God forgives overeating much more quickly than any of those other vices, right? Religion seems to condone food addiction as acceptable, while other addictions are viewed as being sinful. Thus, we had found an acceptable sin and weren't we lucky to find one that seemed to bring so much joy rather than heartache – at least in the moment.

7

That's Gonna Leave a Mark

I run into things. Not with my vehicle, but with my body. I didn't realize the scope of this problem until I was married. My wife learned relatively quickly that I sometimes need some help steering my body or just avoiding things altogether.

As I sat back and thought about it, I began to recall that this propensity for bodily damage due to impact with inanimate devices had plagued me from an early age. It did get worse later in life, and I have a theory as to why, but more on that later.

If you started reading at the beginning of this book, a very good place to start, you may recall that I had several crashes on my Big Wheel before reaching the age of three. I took a fair number of crashes on my regular bicycle, too, as I grew older. But that's normal fare for most kids.

One of my earliest non-Big Wheel/bicycle memories of hurting myself significantly happened when we lived in Iowa. We lived in the church parsonage, which was a huge, rambling old Midwestern house with five bedrooms, a massive kitchen, and multiple basement rooms full of scary things. The house also had a wraparound porch on the front, which was surrounded by yew bushes. My brother, always the more athletic one, discovered there was great fun to be had by running the length of the porch and leaping over the bushes at the end. Like a graceful antelope, he would gallop down the porch, leap into the air with the strength and aplomb of a trained figure skater or ballet dancer, and land surefootedly on the ground on the other side. Occasionally, just for fun, he would end with a forward roll or somersault as he landed.

I watched and thought, "I can do that." It was a thought that common sense should have canceled out. Alas, it did not. It didn't help matters that my brother was egging me on and calling me a wuss for not even trying. "Fine," I thought. "I'll show him."

I began my takeoff roll with all the grace and speed of a 747, which requires at least an 11,000-foot runway to become airborne. I had maybe fifteen feet at my disposal. My chubby little legs accelerated as fast as they could. "Wow," I thought. "I'm not going very fast yet," as the end of the porch drew precipitously near. I leapt and promptly realized my form was as un-antelope and anti-aplomb as could possibly be.

For some reason, my brain must have thought I was ski jumping or water skiing, because I stuck my feet out in front of me…way out in front of me, and landed…HARD, right on my tailbone. I did not roll. I did not somersault. I crash landed.

When the violence of the landing ceased, I realized I couldn't breathe. It's the first time I remember having the wind knocked out of me, but it would certainly not be the last.

I thought I was dying. I gasped for air, positive my lungs had been obliterated by the sheer impact of my maladroit attempt to be cool and athletic like my brother. My brother peered over the edge of the porch.

"Are you OK?"

"I…can't…breathe," I gasped.

"Oh, you probably have the wind knocked out of you. Just wait a minute; it'll come back." He left and went inside to get a popsicle.

I lay on the ground, dying, and asking God to forgive me for all the horrible things I had done in my seven years on earth, especially the bad thoughts I was having about killing my brother.

"That's gonna leave a mark," I thought.

But he was right. A few minutes later, my breath returned, and I got up, went inside, and also got a popsicle. Disaster averted. Amazingly, nothing was broken, except for my pride and perhaps a piece of my tailbone.

A few years later, I was climbing trees with a friend near the toxic waste dump at the edge of our neighborhood. We had been swimming that afternoon in Mama's Hole, our name for the greenish colored pond that filled with rainwater between the mounds of slag from the steel factory.

My wife thinks this name and this pond are disgusting. She's right. But we were young and didn't care or know any better, for that matter. I also don't recall who came up with the ridiculous name or why it was chosen, but it's a name that definitely sticks in a person's mind forever!

For those of you who may never have lived near a toxic waste dump, steel factory, or slag pit, here's a brief description. Slag is what's leftover in the furnaces after they make steel. It's basically stony, glassy, sharp bits of burned out impurities and other lovely chemicals. It's perfect for spreading on your driveway, which is what it was mostly used for when I was a kid.

The steel plant behind our house produced a lot of it and would dump it in huge mounds between our neighborhood boundary and the plant itself. It made a lovely place to ride your bike, sled (during the winter), or store toxic waste barrels full of sludge, which was the other thing the steel plant did on the property. We weren't supposed to be there. No trespassing signs were everywhere.

Mama's Hole provided enough water for a few trees to grow around it. As I recall, they were pines of some type, and a few were quite tall. We climbed them regularly, usually without incident. On this particular day, though, that was all about to change.

I was chasing my friend Lee to the top. He was always faster than I, mostly because he was less than half my size. He could squeeze through areas between the branches that I couldn't, which meant I had to take a longer detour route to get to the top.

As I neared the top, I saw a branch of dubious sturdiness just a bit above where I was standing. It seemed to be the best possibility for reaching the top, but I paused briefly to assess its use as a branch certified to hold a 250-pound teenager. I was skeptical, but I saw no other options.

I cautiously extended my foot and pressed down a bit. It didn't seem to give much. Good sign, I thought. I stepped gingerly onto the branch, hoping and praying it would continue to support me for the brief moment it would take to step up to the next branch, which was much larger and stronger looking.

You would think that my commonsense meter would have kicked in, considering that I was at least forty to fifty feet (best guess) off the ground. Unfortunately, the commonsense meter must reside in the prefrontal cortex of the brain, which we now know doesn't fully develop in adult males until the mid- to late twenties.

SNAP.

The sound of death approaching echoed through the treetops.

I don't remember much of the next ten seconds or so. I think I was screaming, but I'm sure. What I do remember is that I was unceremoniously crashing through branches on my way down. Some gave way better than others. I was grateful for those that decided to give way and sacrifice themselves on my behalf. Not only did it reduce the pain when they gave way, it also helped to slow me down a bit.

THUMP.

I landed on the ground square on my tailbone and promptly laid down. I couldn't breathe. Was my back broken? Was anything broken? Was I dying? Why couldn't I breathe? Then it hit me – the memory of the yew bush debacle. The wind was knocked out of me, again. I would recover. Or so I hoped.

"That's gonna leave a mark," I thought.

Lee scrambled down toward me. "Are you OK?" he asked.

"I...can't...breathe," I gasped. "But it's OK. It's just the wind knocked out of me. Give me a few minutes."

Lee looked momentarily concerned, and then started laughing.

"Dude, what the heck? You should have seen that! It was like watching a whale fall out of the sky!"

I was not amused with his attempt at humor or his lack of attention as to whether I was dying or had broken every bone in my body.

"Shut up," I said.

Eventually, like clockwork, my wind returned, and I gingerly sat upright. Nothing appeared to be broken. In fact, not much hurt at all, although I would later see several bruises from my "branch-friends." Looking around me, I noticed that I had landed right in the middle of a huge pile of pine needles. To this day, I credit those pine needles with saving my life. I've never since underestimated the power of a tree in a toxic waste dump to do good.

As an adult, I continued to have more than my fair share of impacts. I didn't feel like a klutz, but based on my track record, I think I was squarely in that camp. I'd be walking along and minding my own business only to have some object rudely appear out of nowhere and be in my way. On occasion, I'd think I had run into someone instead of something. My wife and a good friend of ours were brought to hysterics when I once apologized to a parking meter after walking right into it and thinking it was someone getting in their car.

The problem seemed to worsen after I lost 230 pounds. I lamented that I had lost my ability to dance, but I should have been more concerned about what was happening to my spatial perception. I felt completely out of sorts with a weird unsteadiness on my feet. Never one to be afraid of heights, I felt like I would topple off a ladder or fall forward and roll off the cliff when I was in a high place. I also started running into more and more things, animate and inanimate.

For some reason, I wouldn't see objects that were easily within the range of my peripheral vision (or central vision, even!) and would walk right into them. I took more than one fall on my bicycle during this era. In fact, one of my riding partners gave up on me because when I went down, she often did as well in an effort to avoid running into me.

At one point, things came to a head (literally) when I was out riding my bike on one of the city's bike trails. Tooling along at a decent pace, I came around a corner and saw a branch hanging low over the trail. A storm had rolled through the night before, and I figured the branch had fallen as a result. I ducked, except I didn't duck enough.

74

WHAM!

My head smashed into the branch and my neck snapped back. Somehow, I managed to stay on the bike and stay upright, but I pulled over as soon as I could stop to consider whether I had seriously injured my neck or not. Miraculously, I felt no pain.

"That's gonna leave a mark," I thought.

I pulled off my bike helmet and saw a huge dent in the upper right quadrant. It wasn't lost on me that the dent probably would have been in my skull if it weren't for the helmet. I have refused to ever ride a bike without a helmet since.

So, what was going on? Well, I don't have hard evidence, but I think my spatial perception was off because I was half the size I had been for many years. My brain needed time to catch up and realize I was only thirty inches (or so) across and not sixty.

I asked a couple scientists about this and whether it had been researched, and they said no. Maybe it's a bunch of hogwash and I'm just genetically a klutz, but it seemed very odd that the number of collisions increased after I lost a large amount of weight. It's amazing that during all the crashes, I've never broken anything. Perhaps it's a testimony to the power of fat to cushion – my own built in bubble wrap!

Sometimes the collisions were not my fault, though, and I feel a need to redeem myself here. Around the time that I was losing so much weight, Lee's sister, Twila, called me and asked if I'd like to join a group of friends for a weekend of fun at a ski resort in northern Michigan. Even though I hate winter and generally don't like outdoor winter activities, I agreed to go. I thought it would be fun to see people and relax around a fire, even if I didn't ski or enjoy riding sleds.

I had been traumatized by sleds as a child. My family had saucer sleds – those round sleds like Chevy Chase rockets down the hill on in *Christmas Vacation*. I always had more speed than the other kids because mass increases velocity. But no matter how hard I tried, I couldn't keep that darn sled facing forward. Inevitably, shortly after launching down the hill, the stupid sled would spin around, and I'd be heading down the hill backwards unable to see people, places or trees in my path. I hated it.

Lee told me the resort had a snow tubing hill. It was basically like sledding, but you sat in a huge inflated rubber innertube. I figured I would have more control, plus they had this gizmo that pulled you and the tube back up the hill, so you didn't have to walk. Sounded like it might possibly have enjoyment potential, so I bought a pair of long underwear and prepared for the trip.

My first couple of trips down the snow tubing hill were uneventful, for the most part. I still had some trouble keeping myself facing forward but figured out if I stuck my boot into the snow, the tube would usually spin back toward the front.

As I was being pulled back up the hill for the third run, I noticed a glare on the snow. It was a busy day and the air temperature hovered right around the freezing mark. Unbeknownst to newbie victims such as myself, the hill had turned to ice as a result.

Lee and Twila's mother, Connie, went down before me. I had known Connie since I was a young kid and thought of her as a second mom. She was loads of fun and often accompanied us on our various adventures. The spotter at the top of the hill saw her disappear and told me to go.

I started my takeoff roll and spun around backwards. I stuck my foot out, but found it hopping and skipping over the ice instead of turning my tube forward. I seemed to be moving much faster, too. As I neared the bottom, I managed to spin partway around and saw Connie struggling to stand up on the ice in front of me.

I looked at her and yelled, "Move, move, move!!!" She spun around and tried to make an escape, but it was too late.

WHAM!

I hit Connie at a high rate of speed flipping her up in the air. She landed face down in the snow. I looked backwards to see if she was OK, but I was dealing with other problems and had to quickly change my focus.

Like a runaway airplane, I was not slowing down on the icy snow. My collision with Connie had barely slowed me at all and my tube kept going at a frightening pace. I recalled there was a large pile of snow at the edge of the tubing area that I assumed was designed to keep runaway tubes from going over the edge of the hill and into the road below. Silly me. I placed my trust in that buffer and stuck my feet out trying to slow myself.

I hit the pile of snow and heard a loud explosion. Snow flew everywhere. I noticed that I was momentarily airborne and then suddenly I slammed down in the road and began sliding toward the ski lodge located at the bottom of the road (the road dead-ended into the entrance area of the lodge). As I landed, I heard a sickening "pop" and realized I was sliding toward the entrance on my butt and not on the tube, which had popped when I landed in the road.

I finally slid to a stop a few feet from the doors of the lodge, which promptly opened for me as the sensor detected my presence. It's a miracle I didn't keep going and slide my way right into the lodge!

"That's gonna leave a mark," I thought. This thought was quickly followed by a wave of embarrassment, as I realized what it must have looked like to see a fat guy break through a snow barrier, pop a tube, and slide up to the entrance of a hotel.

I was still big, even though at the time I had lost 230 pounds. And my feelings of embarrassment about my size and size-related debacles never left, no matter how much weight I lost. I laugh about this experience now, but at the time, I was mortified, and after rescuing Connie, I just wanted to disappear from sight and the inevitable laughter of those who had witnessed that afternoon's crash landing.

8

Maintenance, We Have an Emergency...

The bathroom is not supposed to be a scary place. It is supposed to be a respite, a place of solitude, peace, relief, and contemplative moments – especially for those of us who are lifelong bathroom readers. Most people are grateful for the abundant availability of public restrooms. Public mobility is enhanced by knowing that when nature calls, society has answered, and unless one is traveling across the Mojave Desert (or Wyoming, as I once found out), facilities are available for necessary excretory relief.

For fat people, however, public restrooms are often scary places. Home restrooms can be scary places too, especially when visiting someone and not being familiar with the layout and sturdiness of the facilities. What many take for granted, fat people approach with fear and trembling. To this day, I battle lutropublicaphobia – the fear of public restrooms.

The first obstacle fat people face is size. Consider the type of restrooms available in most gas stations or convenience stores. I am very familiar with these, due to my food addiction, which has taken me to more gas stations and convenience stores than probably anyone other than the vendors that serve them and the employees that work there. Most of these men's restrooms have one or two urinals and one toilet. The urinals are usually at different levels on the wall. One is intended for children but can be used by an adult if necessary. Most men who enter the restroom head to the urinal and take care of business standing up. Enter another significant obstacle for fat men – urinals often don't work. Why?

Most fat men need to lower their pants and their underwear to access the necessary plumbing. This isn't an anatomy book or a horror story, so I'm not going to go into detail. Suffice it to say, there's a lot of fat, skin, and other obstacles IN the way ON the way to the man parts. It's not as easy as simply unzip and go.

Obviously, most fat men (myself included) don't want to be standing at a urinal with their pants around their ankles and their underwear around their knees. Thus, the solution is to use the big toilet – as in the toilet designed for sitting. This leads to the fourth and final obstacle – access.

There's usually only one of these toilets, and often, it's in use by a skinny person conducting a longer transaction. Fat people also lack the ability to hold it very well, meaning that when you have to go, you have to go. I've done many a potty dance while waiting for access to the big toilet.

Occasionally, there may be more than one big toilet. In these situations, there's usually a handicap stall (nice and wide; big enough for a wheelchair) and a smaller stall. A new dilemma now emerges. Using the smaller stall is difficult. In some situations, I encountered a stall so narrow, I would have to turn sideways to get in, and then suck in and turn the other direction to shut the door.

At the same time, I'm not officially handicapped, even though being extremely fat can handicap a person in myriad ways, and I felt an obligation to leave the big stall open in case someone came in who was. Decisions, decisions…usually, I made my decision based on who was present, the urgency to go, and just plain practicality. There were some stalls that simply left me no option but to use the handicap stall.

You may be wondering what happens if a fat person actually has to use the sit-down toilet. This is a particularly frightening situation. If I found myself in an area where I didn't know the restrooms, I would generally pray or head to a facility that I knew usually had a one-person bathroom; you know, the kind with a lock on the door that only allows one person access to the facility at a time.

Fat people are gassy. Fat people often have explosive diarrhea. I know you are just thrilled to find that out, but it's the truth. You can't eat 10,000 calories of junk food, fast food, greasy donuts, burgers, fries, etc. without having it impact what comes out the other end. No one, and I mean NO ONE, wants to be present at the moment yesterday's binge chooses to make an exit.

If a one-person facility was not available, I would use the flush method to cover any noise. Public restroom toilets are usually pretty loud when they flush. I would strategically time the noisiest part of the flush to cover up the loud sounds. Sometimes, lack of flexibility was an issue, and I couldn't quite manage. In those situations, I prayed for a loud hand dryer and would take advantage of that cover-up noise.

If I was forced into the smaller stall, more calisthenics were required. It was simply a matter of physics; most toilet stalls have fixed walls. If a person is wider than the available space, this creates a dilemma.

Many times the available space was further reduced by the intrusion of the toilet paper roll. I learned to hate many of those dispensers over the years because it was often the acrobatics it took to get around them that could be the most vexing. On many occasions, I was left sitting at some crazy angle with the toilet paper roll pressing tightly against my side. Perhaps the most unfortunate reality of this situation was it made it VERY difficult to sit comfortably. Truthfully, there were plenty of times when I nearly made myself sick to avoid using a public restroom. That's how emotionally draining the experience of draining physically could be.

There were other problems that could arise unexpectedly. Probably the most common was the broken toilet seat. I have broken so many toilet seats in my life, I can't possibly put a number on it. Many of those seats were at home. At the moment when I would lean or shift my weight, the toilet seat would crack under the immense burden of my girth.

Usually, this resulted in a distinguishable thud that I came to recognize over time. On occasion, the crack would open enough that some of my skin would work itself in, and I would receive a horrible pinch. My mom grew weary of replacing toilet seats, so when I got my first job, she mandated it was my responsibility to take care of any broken toilet seats. I spent a significant amount of my minimum-wage dollars replacing toilet seats.

I did break a few seats in public restrooms also. I hate to admit it, but when that occurred, I usually left as quickly as possible without saying a word. It probably wasn't the Christian thing to do, but I just couldn't bring myself to approach the counter and admit that I had broken their toilet seat. As if all this trauma weren't enough, there are a few other public restroom incidents that contributed to my lifelong fear.

Virtually no one enjoys the experience of using an airplane restroom. For a fat person, it borders on torture. Flying is already an anxiety-laden experience. Anxiety often contributes to issues resulting in the need to use the bathroom…frequently.

I quickly developed techniques to try and avoid having to use an airplane bathroom. I wouldn't drink anything for at least four hours before my flight. I would take four doses of anti-diarrheal medicine. I would refuse to drink anything on the plane. These measures typically worked, unless it was a particularly long flight. These methods also meant I usually arrived at my destination weak and dehydrated. It was a price I was willing to pay.

On one occasion, I had no choice but to get up and go. I headed to the back of the plane (an ordeal in and of itself – stupid narrow airplane aisles!), pushed open the door, and assessed the probability that my body would fit into the dimensions in front of me. Convinced there was hope, I stepped inside. My stomach was up against the back of the toilet, and my butt was hanging out slightly into the aisle. I somehow managed to suck it in and pull the door shut.

If I was going to be successful, I decided my only hope was to get my pants down, lean forward and balance myself with one hand against the fuselage, while the other hand guided my man parts in the direction of the hole. With a bit of grunting, pushing, sweating, muttering, and a whole lot of sucking it in, I managed to get the stream going, with most of it headed toward the hole.

Then, the turbulence struck. Why Lord, why then? Why during a perfectly smooth flight did the turbulence have to occur at the exact moment I manage to get everything operational? The plane lurched and bucked violently. I fell back against the door, which flew open revealing my bare butt to the back of the plane. Thank goodness I am relatively certain only one very shocked flight attendant saw me, and I managed to stumble back into the restroom quickly before drawing additional attention. My heart breaks for that poor flight attendant. I'm sure she had nightmares for weeks. I was too embarrassed to even look at her for the rest of the flight.

The plane seemed to hit smooth air again, and I pulled up my pants (banging my head on the fuselage) and started the process of once again turning around to exit the bathroom. That's when I realized something felt damp. Oh no. What had happened? Apparently during the violent lurching and bucking, I had forgotten to stop my stream and had managed to pee right down my leg and onto my pants.

Now what? Realizing there was no good solution, I determined the best course of action was to return to my seat as quickly as possible. I tried to pretend nothing was wrong. I'm glad I was moving toward people from behind, rather than toward their faces. I did my best to turn sideways and not brush against anyone as I made my way back to my seat. Thankfully, the flight was long enough that my pants mostly dried by the time we landed.

The second episode nearly resulted in me swearing off public restrooms completely. It occurred at a highway rest area somewhere in the northern reaches of Michigan. It was a pretty isolated location, which is a good thing. I was also by myself, which is another good thing, because there were no actual witnesses.

I had stopped to eat something huge and hideous several miles before at the civilized outpost and was now dealing with the onset of intense diarrhea, courtesy of my lack of a gall bladder. Nearly all extremely fat people who have been fat for a substantial portion of their lives end up having their gall bladders removed. I'm not a physician, but based on my experience and what I have read, it's most likely because of heavy fat and cholesterol intake resulting in the formation of gallstones or a diseased organ.

One particularly lovely side effect of having no gall bladder is drop syndrome. This extremely unpleasant experience generally occurs when a long period of time has passed without eating, and then a large amount of food enters the digestive tract. If the food is greasy, the impact is even more substantial.

The best way I know to describe drop syndrome is to think of a drain. I can actually feel the valves in my stomach opening and the food making a quick exit from my stomach to my digestive tract. This is often accompanied by very loud noises. Friends who have been present when this occurs have mentioned that my face often becomes white as a sheet, and I break out in a sweat.

There is a distinct feeling of suction, just like what you observe with water going down a drain. Again, the laws of physics apply, and with that much food and stomach fluids entering your lower digestive tract so quickly, a person has literally seconds to find a toilet before an explosion of epic proportions occurs.

I pulled into the rest area at a high rate of speed, grateful to be lucky enough to be so close to one in such a desolate area. I was also a bit afraid because of the remoteness. Rest areas in remote places can be freaky places. I ran inside with my butt cheeks squeezed together, and what I saw caused immediate trauma.

The facilities were pretty ugly, and because it was so remote, it had that distinct out-house feel to it. Smells were potent, bugs were prevalent, and it wasn't in the best condition overall. It was also old. The urinals and the toilet, as I would soon find out, were made from aluminum.

I rushed toward the stall, yanked open the door, and assessed the situation. Everything appeared to be okay, except I briefly noted the back of the toilet wasn't flush with the wall. As with most public toilets, the part of the toilet a person sits on was bolted to the wall. It was the bolts that I would later blame for not holding up their end of the bargain.

By this time, sweat was pouring off my face, and I knew I was going to have to use this toilet, even if it wasn't in the best condition. I spun around, yanked down my pants and sat down.

At first, everything seemed to be fine. Suddenly, I felt a violent lurching and heard a distinct crack. I tumbled forward, smacked my head on the toilet paper dispenser (also made of aluminum) and realized I was now nearly on the floor with my legs sprawled in front of me and nasty water running down the floor and right into my pants.

Yes, folks, the toilet had snapped off the wall. I don't think it broke completely, thanks to plumbing, but it now tilted down toward the floor. The contents, which just moments before I had been so relieved to get rid of, now raced toward my pants. This all happened in a matter of seconds, and I was in a bit of shock.

After coming to my senses and taking note of the fact that I now had soaked pants, I jumped up (as quickly as a 400-plus pound person can jump) and pulled my pants out of the flood. I was horrified, mortified, and utterly caught off guard. Now what was I going to do? My pants were soaked with nasty toilet water!

At this point, the remoteness of the location became the blessing. Realizing no one was around, and hoping that no one would be around anytime soon, I headed to the sink. I managed to rinse out and kind of wash my pants, at least to the point where I could probably get by until I got home. I spent another twenty minutes standing in front of the hand dryer in my underpants.

This was a tedious, but necessary process. My only other recourse would have been to make a mad dash to my car in my underwear and hope that no one would notice I had no pants as I made the four-hour trip back home. The dryer helped, and that, along with a spare blanket I had in the car, kept my seat from getting soaked. Disaster averted again. Praise the Lord.

You would think that would be the last story. It's only one of probably a dozen or more. Earlier in this enlightening essay, I mentioned drop syndrome and the unfortunate side effects of gall bladder removal. Nothing I had previously endured prepared me for what happened the evening after that surgical procedure.

I was only fifteen years old when I had my gall bladder removed. I was the youngest person to ever have the procedure at the local hospital, thanks to my horrible diet and obese lifestyle that wreaked havoc on the poor and innocent organ. Thankfully, gall bladder surgery had recently been updated to a procedure using small, laser-like instruments rather than the twelve- to fourteen-inch incision it had taken previously. Recovery time in the hospital dropped from nearly two weeks to usually two days or fewer.

After surgery, I was resting in my hospital bed. My mom was with me and I wanted her to stay overnight. I wanted my mommy. At fifteen, some guys still want their mommies, especially when they feel like they've just been punched repeatedly in the gut. The doctor and my mom didn't think it was necessary for her to stay overnight, though, so my mom left shortly after dinner.

At this point in the story, it's important to paint a bit of a picture of what the room and I looked like. I was wearing the traditional hospital gown, except my version wasn't large enough to cover my rear. Thus, when I got up to do anything such as use the restroom or take a brief post-surgical walk, I couldn't close the rear gap, and my bare butt was exposed to the world.

I was also hooked up to an IV which was hanging from a cart next to my bed. Shortly before my mother left, a fateful decision had been made by the nurse. In an effort to create more room on the side of the bed where she would stand to take my vitals, she moved the IV cart to the other side of the bed. No one, especially me, had a clue on how fateful of a decision that would be.

I ate my bland dinner and settled back in bed for what I was sure would be a mostly sleepless night. It's impossible for a 300-pound teenager to get comfortable in a hospital bed when confined to his back.

About fifteen minutes after I ate, I began to feel the first rumbles in my gut. They intensified, and suddenly I realized I was about to experience the mother of all diarrhea explosions. Hospital staff had neglected to tell me about drop syndrome, or the fact that during initial recovery from gall bladder surgery, horrendous diarrhea is quite common as the digestive system adjusts to life without a gall bladder.

At first, I didn't panic because I figured I had time to get out of bed, which took slightly longer than usual due to just having had surgery, but still wasn't overly difficult. It was then I realized the decision to move the IV cart was most unfortunate. The cart had been moved to the side of the bed opposite from the side facing the restroom. No big deal, I thought. I'll just wheel it back around the end of the bed and walk it into the restroom with me as planned.

There were two very important factors that sealed my fate. First, I failed to realize that after the IV cart was moved, the large, couch-like structure that was available for family to sit or sleep on had also been moved up against the opposite side of the cart.

Second, I had no idea how intensely the diarrhea was going to demand a rapid exit.

I walked around the end of the bed, grabbed the cart, and realized that as the feet of the cart approached the gap between the bed and the couch, there wasn't enough room for the wheels to roll between the two. Suddenly, I began to panic. Now what?

At this point, my stomach was in full scale rebellion, and I was squeezing my butt cheeks together for all they were worth to try and keep things in check until I made it to the toilet. I struggled with the cart... unsuccessfully. I tried to move the couch but had immediate feelings of extreme pain in my gut and realized it probably wasn't a good idea to move heavy objects the evening after surgery. For a moment, I explored the idea of swinging the IV cart up and over the bed but realized that was likely also an exercise in futility for a recently wounded man.

I was trapped. Bad things were about to happen.

I reached for the call light and began to shout for help. It was too late. I had been squeezing my cheeks and praying for anal restraint as long as I could, but nature took its course. A huge jet of diarrhea shot out of my rear (keep in mind, my butt was uncovered, thanks to the too-small surgical gown) flew across the room and hit the wall, where it began a slow descent toward the floor. Once the floodgate opened, there was no holding back.

Another jet shot out and hit a nearby lamp with a distinct sizzling sound as it landed on the light bulb. I began to heave and buck violently as I realized there was no hope left for controlling what was happening. All the pent-up surgical waste, the bland dinner, what seemed like a gallon or more of bile that was no longer stored in my gall bladder but instead deposited in my stomach seemed to jettison out of me with the force of a fire hose.

Shortly thereafter, the nurse arrived. I'm not sure if it was the call light, the shouts, or the strange grunts and moans that finally got her attention, but she entered the room and a look of absolute horror gathered on her face. "My God, you crapped all over everything!" she said.

I looked at her helplessly. Suddenly, as if the trauma I had just endured weren't enough, I realized that I recognized her face. Small town syndrome... at the worst possible moment. I sat next to her son in the band at my school, and her son was one of the more substantial bullies in my life at that time.

I began to cry. I apologized profusely. I explained the dilemma. I tried to point out how I was trapped. There was nothing I could do. All this crying and apologizing took place in the midst of a growing puddle on the floor, which was soon followed by an overwhelming olfactory assault. Once she recovered from the shock, the nurse sprang into action, and there were soon several staff in the room cleaning up the walls, the lamp, the floor, the pictures, and me.

The next morning, the new nurse greeted me with a sly grin on her face. "You sure were the topic of discussion last night," she said. "We've never had an experience quite like that one."

I responded languidly, "and I'm sure you hope to never have one like that again."

"That's for sure," she said. "And you know what? What's crazy about the whole thing is they were supposed to remove your IV about an hour before that occurred but were behind and figured it was no big deal. You definitely ensured that it was a HUGE deal," she laughed.

I did not reciprocate. I was mortified. And as expected, when I went back to school, my dear "friend" had already managed to share my experience (with his own spin, of course) with everyone else (life before HIPAA, unfortunately). Oh, the inhumanity of it all!

One of the most relieving aspects of losing weight was when all the stress and trauma around public restroom use was gone. I could stand up and go at any urinal, no problem. I could fit in any stall and not be concerned the toilet was going to break off the wall! It may sound strange, especially if you've never been extremely overweight, but it was incredibly liberating to be just like nearly everyone else walking into a public restroom and realizing the issue was more about cleanliness than sturdiness.

Some scars are deep, though, and I still deal with public restroom phobia. I have learned to motivate myself to stay healthy in many ways, and one of those is to remind myself of those days of continual bathroom trauma, and how wonderful it would be to never have to "go there" again.

9

Planes, Trains and Automobiles

Fat people fear getting from Point A to Point B. This fear is especially profound when it involves someone else's car, an airplane, public transportation, or a bicycle.

As a kid, travel and transportation weren't terribly traumatic. Riding an airplane was a thrill. Even a fat kid like me didn't have too much trouble fitting into those skinny seats. After all, I was eight years old with a 36-inch waist, which is comparable to an average grown male. All of that changed as an adult.

The bike wasn't too much of an issue either, except I popped more tires and certain parts of the bike were more prone to breakage. I seemed to always inherit my older brother's hand-me-down bikes, which meant some of them were pretty beat up even before they had to endure my extra weight. One bike I inherited had the banana seat that was so popular during those days. All was good until I was jumping off a ramp, and the two support bars at the back busted right off. After that, there was nothing to hold up the rear of the seat, but I really didn't care. I continued to ride that bike for another couple of years with the added task of balancing the seat.

I purchased my first car from a friend of our family and deacon in our church for $350. The year was 1993, and the car was a 1985 Chevy Cavalier. The Cavalier, often referred to as "the beer can of cars," was in dire straits in many regards when I bought it. However, it ran and served my purposes well. Plus, the person I purchased it from let me work off the bill by helping him around his shop and willingly kept the Cavalier running for me throughout high school.

At that time, I weighed about three hundred pounds. Remarkably, the Cavalier's seatbelt fit me, but I did bust two seats. Yes, I know it may be hard to imagine, but fat people bust a lot of seats. Cars like the Cavalier, and probably many others, were not built with sturdy enough plastic to handle three hundred or more pounds.

On both occasions, as I reached for the seatbelt, putting excess pressure on the back of the seat, it simply snapped and the seatback broke, falling backwards into the back seat. Try explaining that to the local junk yard without your face turning red! Somehow, I managed to do it and became pretty adept at swapping out seats in my Cavalier!

By the time I graduated from high school, I was concerned that I might have to get a seat belt extender. If you've never read the owner's manual that comes with your vehicle you may not even be aware that such a device exists. Apparently, seat belt extenders have been around since the time of the federal government's requirement that all vehicles have seat belts. I'm quite certain that requests for the device were very infrequent in the early years of seat belt usage. With America's obesity epidemic, seatbelt extenders became more widely used. Eventually, the auto industry realized what was occurring, and most cars now come with ample seat belts for nearly every girth.

Fortunately, the two vehicles that I owned after the Cavalier had automatic seatbelts, which meant they had a motorized shoulder strap that would run back and forth along a track along the door sill. An additional blessing of this briefly lived invention was the extra fabric (i.e. length) built into the belt because it had to move out of the way and give even skinny people enough room to get in and out of the vehicle without being asphyxiated by a strap wrapped around their necks.

Near the end of my ownership of the second vehicle, I outgrew even the extra fabric, which caused an unusual situation. I had noticed that the seat belt seemed to be having a more and more difficult time closing around me, but I didn't think much about it (teenage cluelessness, I suppose). Finally, the limit must have been reached. As I started the car one day, the motorized seatbelt began its sojourn, and about an inch from the end, it began squealing and bucking, and I smelled smoke.

I stopped the car, but I was trapped. The seat belt motor had burned up, the track had been stripped, and when I opened the door to escape, the formerly automatic seatbelt was no longer automatic. Thankfully, a lawyer or an engineer had realized the possibility of trapped occupants, and the emergency release mechanism saved the day.

And so began my foray into several years of seat belt hell. The next vehicle I purchased had regular seatbelts that did not fit. I contacted the dealership, and they ordered a seatbelt extender. When it arrived, I was astounded to see that the extender was almost three feet long! When I attempted to use it, the actual buckle mechanism ended up falling in the valley right between my man boobs, which did not feel like the best location to absorb energy during a crash!

I improvised. I tied the fabric into several knots to reduce the length and called it good. Thankfully, I never had a crash, but still wonder about the dubious safety of my improvised seatbelt extender.

The other insidious thing about seat belt extenders is there is no such thing as a universal model. Vehicles come with a plethora of seatbelt latches, and sharing seatbelt extenders across vehicle models (even within the same manufacturer) is generally not possible. I found this out the hard way. Thinking there must be some kind of universal law governing seat belt latches, I figured every car was the same. I picked up my free extender from the dealership and devised ways to hide it if I had to ride in someone else's car.

An embarrassing learning experience occurred when I had to go to Detroit with one of my coworkers. I snuck the extender into my coat pocket. When I got in the car, I tried to discreetly latch it in. No luck. It wouldn't connect. Of course, the mad dance I was doing in the front seat trying to get the dang thing to work drew my coworker's attention. He seemed like a nice guy, so I just told him. We both took a look and soon realized the tongue part on the end of my extender was not the same as the tongue on the end of his seatbelt. Now what?

I prayed, sucked it in as hard as I could, and tried to get that seatbelt around me. I figured Detroit was only an hour or so away from Lansing, and I could go without a normal amount of air for that long. Still no luck. At this point, I was faced with the decision of whether it was safe to ride to Detroit with no seatbelt. My chances of getting shot (always a distinct possibility in Detroit) were probably more significant than getting in an accident, so I decided not to worry about it too much. While I was mulling over my concerns that my coworker might get a ticket, we discovered another problem.

The car sounded a loud and annoying beep every twenty seconds or so if the seatbelt wasn't fastened. Most modern vehicles are seat-belt nanny equipped. There was no way we were going to put up with that all the way to Detroit, so I thought for a minute, and pulled the seatbelt behind me and buckled it. Problem solved, again.

Realizing this was going to be an ongoing problem, I eventually developed various ways of dealing with it. The most common was to rush to the car before my coworkers or friends, pray that it was unlocked, and then quickly latch the seatbelt behind me, but grab the front belt and pull it over me so it looked like I was buckled in. Welcome to the amazing world of fat man seatbelt usage techniques. Sometimes you do what you gotta do to save face.

I had other embarrassing moments in cars, too. My friend Jared and I used to really enjoy tooling around the countryside, especially in the summer. Since Jared is six five, we rarely tooled around in my Cavalier. If you've never seen a six foot five man who weighs more than three hundred pounds in the passenger seat of a Cavalier, use your imagination. It wasn't a pretty sight.

We had a solution, though. Jared had the coolest car I had ever seen. His Uncle Bohac had given him his 1970 Chevy Nova with a 3-speed column shifter when he no longer had any use for it. It was bright blue, with blue vinyl seats and only had about 30,000 miles on it. Jared wasn't very fond of driving it, finding the transmission to be cantankerous due to a linkage in need of a lube job. I, on the other hand, was enamored with it. I begged Jared to let me drive it every chance I got. He usually relented, and I became the chauffeur on our frequent donut runs.

On one particularly warm, spring day, Jared and I were returning from the Chapin General Store loaded down with Little Debbie's and some antique canned green beans Jared had spied on the shelf. Chapin was a town even smaller than Carland located about five miles to the north. Unlike Carland, Chapin's original general store continued to operate. Stepping into it was like walking into 1920. While some current food and drink was always available, the shelves were never cleaned, emptied or rotated. So, it was a hidden antique paradise. Jared and I frequented it regularly, looking for that rare can of 1952 green beans to fill the void between 1951 and 1953.

As we headed back south to Carland, I was at the helm of the Nova. Normally, due to its age and heft, we kept the Nova to fifty miles per hour or less. However, I was feeling a bit cheeky, enjoying the spring breeze blowing through the side window vents (remember those?) which we had opened for the first time since winter. I found myself pushing the Nova up to sixty, and then maybe closer to seventy, relishing in that delicious breeze.

I suddenly realized we were fast approaching The Dip. The Dip was a chronic depression in the road on the southbound side. It had been there as long as I could remember and probably as long as the road itself. Periodically, it would wash out in a storm and the county would dutifully come out to repair the road without ever fixing the root cause.

I don't know enough about classic cars to relate the entire suspension setup of a 1970 Chevy Nova. I am aware enough of how cars operate to know that a disaster was pending. The Nova rode like a barge because it WAS a land-based barge. Saying the suspension was soft is a gross understatement.

Becoming increasingly aware of the fast-approaching doomsday scenario, I braced myself, also realizing that the springs in the Nova's vinyl bench front seat were not likely to offer much assistance in reducing the motion of two three-hundred-plus pound high school boys. As if all these thoughts racing through my head weren't concerning enough, I also realized there was a car in the northbound lane making it impossible for me to swerve around The Dip.

WHAM!!!

We hit The Dip at about sixty-five miles per hour. The front of the car slammed downward with the tires making contact with the top of the wheel wells. The back rose upward, heaven bound, which is where I was certain we were going to be next. As I suspected, Jared and I rose up off the seats, having not bothered to buckle the lap-belt-only seatbelts. Jared hit the ceiling first; he's at least six inches taller than I. I held the steering wheel in a literal death grip, which may have helped keep my noggin' from hitting the ceiling. We both let loose a stream of less-than-Christian speech.

In the midst of all this chaos, I heard a loud metallic SNAP as the rear leaf springs broke and separated from the body of the car. The rear slammed back down against the frame popping both rear tires.

"OMG…we're going to die!!!" screamed Jared.

I was desperately trying to maintain some kind of control. The car's woefully inadequate drum brakes didn't seem to be doing much despite my attempts to pump the pedal as vigorously as I had pumped anything in my entire life. Miraculously, I somehow managed to keep the car more or less on the road and in our lane until we passed the northbound car. As the braking began to have some effect, the car began to spin, most likely due to the popped tires and broken suspension.

I looked over, briefly, at Jared, who was digging his fingernails into the soft plastic dashboard and hyperventilating vigorously. He also appeared to be choking on his own screams.

Thirty or so seconds later, it was all over. The car came to a stop facing the opposite direction toward the pile of miscellaneous suspension parts strewn about in the road. The northbound car's hazard lights blinked ominously in the distance. I had some momentary concern they may have driven over some of the Nova's parts in the road resulting in damage to their car, but as the driver approached, it was clear that he was more worried about us.

I turned and looked at Jared. He turned, wide-eyed, and burst out laughing hysterically. "I peed my pants," said Jared.

"You better check and make sure it was only pee," I said, worried about the condition of my own drawers.

Unfortunately, this encounter with The Dip spelled the end of our adventures in the Nova. The broken leaf springs revealed that the entire frame was rusted and in danger of collapsing. The Nova joined the other scrap cars in the field behind Jared's house. But hang on! Jared and I had even more interesting car experiences. It was always a fun ride for the pair of us.

After Jared stopped driving the Nova, his family acquired a vintage Chevy Malibu. Again, it had belonged to an elderly person and had low miles, but a body of dubious quality. Jared came over one summer afternoon and picked me up for a trip to Lansing.

On the way there, I kept smelling smoke. It was a faint smell, not overly strong and hinting slightly of electrical fire. We had the radio on, so thinking that perhaps it was shorting out, I reached forward to turn it off. We arrived in Lansing, did whatever it was we were doing, and then headed for home. The smoke smell seemed to be getting more intense.

As we took the exit to leave the highway, I looked down and I saw a column of smoke rising between my legs. I lifted my feet and got Jared's attention. "Stop the car! Something's on fire!"

Jared pulled off to the side of the road and hopped out. He didn't see the smoke, and I think he wondered if I had been imagining things. He opened my door, reached down, and pulled back the floor mat. Flames, of massive size (or at least, so it seemed), rose up between my legs. Jared screamed. I peed my pants. I jumped out of the car and started pulling out bits of burning carpet from around the flames. Somehow, I managed to pull enough out to stop the fire, and we both leaned in to inspect the damage.

Where my feet had been resting previously, there was now an open hole. The exhaust manifold was clearly visible, as was a significant part of pavement under the car. Putting two and two together, we realized that the floorboard on that section of the car did not exist. A victim of rust and Michigan's salty roads, it had apparently left the world a long time ago. My short and stubby legs, along with my girth, had been pressing the carpet down against the exhaust manifold. Jared and other members of his family never had that problem because they are so tall; their feet rested far forward of the manifold.

The drive home after the fire was extinguished was interesting indeed. With a giant hole in the floor and the hot manifold exposed to the interior, I had to turn sideways and lean against the door. The dirt, the stones, the sticks, the cigarette butts, and all the other trash on the road was flying in through the hole and making it difficult to breathe. Somehow, we made it home. We both figured the car was done for, but after some thought, Jared had an ingenious plan.

Jared worked at a pizza shop. They used aluminum pizza pans and were just about to get rid of some that were past their useable life. Jared snagged a few, and over the course of a few days, nailed and bolted them to the floor. After that, my feet rested on top of pizza pans, and the interior had a distinctly saucy smell.

I felt a bit guilty about the demise of both the Nova and the Malibu. Whenever unusual things happened that could be related to my weight, I had a tendency to blame myself. If Jared and I had not weighed over six hundred pounds combined, would the Nova's suspension have survived? If I weren't so fat and didn't have such stubby legs, would the Malibu disaster have been averted? Guilt and shame were emotions that came to me quickly, even amid circumstances that seemed outwardly pretty hilarious.

Last, but certainly not least – what led to my decision to purchase the aforementioned Cavalier. My friend Jenna had recently acquired her driver's license. The state of Michigan must not have been aware of what they had just done. Her parents didn't seem to realize the problem either, until after multiple accidents in less than a year.

As happens on occasion in Michigan, a snowstorm moved in during the school day. School officials decided to close school early and get everyone home before the weather worsened. I didn't yet have my license, and usually rode the bus home. On this particular day, Jenna offered to give me a ride, and Jared hopped in as well.

Jared and I knew about some of Jenna's driving history, so we decided to buckle the seatbelts in the rear where we were sitting. Keep in mind that in this era, rear seat belts were only for the lap, and most people did not wear them. It must have been God at work, because it didn't take very long before we were glad those seatbelts were in use.

Jenna seemed rather oblivious to the road conditions. As we left the school and headed down the first road, she accelerated to sixty miles per hour, and I noticed a distinct swaying feeling in the rear of the car. I should have said something but kept silent because it had been so nice of her to offer me a ride.

We turned on to the second street, and I can't say with certainty, but it seemed like Jenna floored the accelerator. The car gained speed rapidly, and the swaying motion began in earnest. Jared looked at me. I looked at him. Fear was in both of our eyes.

Sure enough, the swaying soon gave way to full figure eights in the middle of the road. The car spun around wildly. Jenna was both laughing and screaming, all at the same time. I felt like it was the scene from *Planes, Trains and Automobiles*... you know, the one where Steve Martin sees John Candy as the devil?

Jared was screaming, and cussing, and covering his head, and shouting, "We're going to DIE!!!" I was in so much shock, I think I just sat there trying to protect myself until the car flew into the ditch on the opposite side of the road facing the opposite direction. It's amazing that I didn't pee my pants. Thank God we were on a part of the road where there were no trees, or we surely would have sustained horrible injuries or even death.

The car was on its side in the bottom of a six- to eight-foot deep ditch. From my vantage point, I couldn't even see the road above us. That's how deep in the ditch we were.

After we all regained our senses and realized where we were, we decided to exit the vehicle. I wondered if people passing by would be able to see us if we didn't get out of the car. Getting out of cars is a process that is rarely simple for any fat person even when the vehicle is parked correctly but was especially difficult with the car on its side with the passenger doors against the bottom of the ditch.

Jenna and Jared opened the doors on the driver's side of the car, and Jenna, who weighed about ninety-five pounds, easily

103

crawled out. The ditch wasn't as deep as it seemed from inside the vehicle, so the road was closer than I thought. Jenna held Jared's door open, and he stepped on me (an interesting experience in and of itself) and managed to heave himself out of the car. Jenna's sister, who also weighed only ninety-five pounds and was in the front passenger seat crawled out after Jenna. That left yours truly.

I had no one to step on for additional height or leverage. I had to try and crawl out of the car using just my own body strength. It didn't work. I pulled with all my might on the door frame, but I couldn't grasp anything enough to slither out of the car. Jared tried pulling on my arms, but that didn't work either. For one thing, it was very slippery where he stood, so he couldn't get much traction. For another thing, I weighed more than three hundred pounds at the time, and even though Jared is strong, he isn't that strong! I was trapped.

After several minutes of grunting, strategizing, and praying (on my part), we gave up. I was going to have to stay in the car until a tow truck arrived. At least I was protected from the elements. This was in the pre-cell phone era, which meant Jenna had to walk to the nearest house to call her parents. It didn't take long for them to arrive along with a tow truck. Now, the really embarrassing part got underway.

The tow truck operator didn't want to pull the car out of the ditch with me in it. I imagine the concern was liability if the car were to shift violently, or if something went wrong. A decision was finally made to lower the tow hook into the car where I was able to grasp it and hold on long enough for them to pull me up and out enough that I could get on solid ground and make it the rest of the way.

Yes folks, I was towed out of a car by a tow truck because I was too fat to pull myself out on my own. Jared thought it was hysterically funny. I am so glad it was before cell phones, because I can only imagine the pictures that might have appeared on social media.

Riding in cars is not the only traumatic transportation experience for fat people, however. Flying on an airplane often requires extremely careful planning, Valium, or both. My plane trauma is not because of any closet aerophobia or limited exclusively to the previously mentioned adventures in an airplane restroom. It relates directly to the size of the seat, and the length of the seatbelt. Both these factors induced anxiety at a level relatively close to that of a true phobia.

The easiest solution was to make sure that I never flew alone, so I took any and all steps necessary to ensure that I sat next to a friend or family member, hopefully on a two-seat side of the aisle. Three-seat configurations induced both hope and fear. The hope was that the middle seat might be empty, thus allowing more breathing room for me and my companion. It also meant I could use the fold-down tray of the empty middle seat, since my own tray was more of a bib. It didn't make it more than a couple inches beyond the latch. The fear, of course, was that some stranger would be stuck in the middle, or even worse, I would be stuck in the middle. Thus, when flying on a three-seat configured plane, I always attempted to use the "empty middle seat" method.

Most of the time, this "never-fly-alone" system worked fairly well. Of course, my friend or family member might have a different opinion. Especially my friend Lee, who often traveled with me to various vacation destinations. Lee is about the size of a pencil. He sacrificed at least half of his seat for my benefit. What a guy.

Occasionally, my system failed. Usually, that occurred on work-related trips. With the advent of the Internet, I would search the plane repeatedly right up to the minute of check-in to try and find a seat next to an empty seat. Sometimes this worked, and sometimes it backfired greatly, as it did on one fateful trip to New York City. I noticed as time went on, that both the "never-fly-alone" and "empty middle seat" methods seemed to fail more often. I was perplexed, but soon realized I was not the only person using these methodologies, especially as airlines began honing their sardine-packing skills.

The fateful New York trip occurred in 2005 on a fun vacation with my friends Char and Gwen. Char was roughly the size of a minibus, whereas I was the size of a Greyhound. Using my finely tuned methods, we had agreed that we would both squeeze into a two-seat aisle. Unfortunately for our friend Gwen, the plane on the way to NYC was the feared three-seat configuration. Gwen willingly (I think) sat between us. The flight attendants had no idea that she was there. They skipped over her completely, as she wasn't visible between the two of us.

We made it, and surprisingly, Gwen still liked us. I was so stressed out from the experience that I ate an entire sandwich at the Carnegie Deli shortly after we arrived. If you've ever been to the Carnegie, you know what a feat that was, even for a dude the size of a Greyhound.

On the return flight, we arrived at the airport to find the flight was overbooked. I still held out hope for one of my methods and was encouraged when I noticed upon checking in at the kiosk that the very last row of the plane indeed had an empty seat in the middle. I promptly moved Char and myself to that location –

one of us on each side of the empty seat. The plane boarded, we took our seats, and thought we had outsmarted the system.

Five minutes later, things went terribly wrong. An extremely obese gentleman, probably one hundred pounds or more heavier than I, came down the aisle (sideways of course) arrived at our spot, looked at us, and said, "this must be somebody's idea of a sick joke." You ain't kidding. We had no choice. The plane was full. There were no empty seats. He had attempted my methods as well. We had both failed miserably.

I still don't really know how the three of us managed to fit in that row. I do know that I took the window seat, Char took the middle (bless her soul), and our new fat buddy took the aisle. I was literally jammed against the window and had no room to move. When flight attendants came through to pass out drinks, I had to hold mine flush against the fuselage. Char could barely breathe. Char also suffered from a weak bladder. You can imagine how that doubled or tripled my fear. Thankfully, she managed to keep it together for the duration of the flight.

As the plane took off, our friend Gwen, blissfully seated with two of our skinnier travel companions, turned around in her seat and said, "We're leaning to the left!!!" I laughed, because laughter is usually much easier to deal with in public situations than tears. I'm very glad we chose to skip the Mexican food before that flight. I'm sure Char and our row companion were equally grateful.

Public transportation, especially if it's crowded, is another anxiety-laden experience for fat people and can require extreme panic-attack prevention measures. I've lost track of how many trains, buses, or subways I've been on in large cities in the United States where all eyes have turned my way with a look of fear as I've approached. Seats that are designed for a 36-inch rear don't accommodate a 60-inch rear very well. There's going to be hangover. The question is, will the hangover rob space from someone else, or block the aisle? I usually went with the aisle.

In European cities, the problem is exacerbated even more because by nature of being European, no 60-inch rears exist. There's no need to verify citizenship because without even opening my mouth to talk, it's abundantly clear that I am American by virtue of my girth. Thankfully, trains are usually not an issue, as many of the older trains have a bench-seat setup. Newer trains, such as the Eurostar, are safe, usually, by following one of the methods I used on airplanes. Subways, however, can be an interesting experience.

For example, on a trip to London, my wife and I were crammed into an early morning subway car that literally placed my face right in someone else's armpit, and my butt right in someone else's face. It gave us a whole new perspective on the cheerful voice telling us to "mind the gap."

There seems to be a pervasive fear in Europe that a fat person might explode. Truth be told, I've experienced this phenomenon periodically in the States too, but it's much more common in Europe. Fat people can have some gross body dynamics but exploding isn't one of them. In close quarters such as that subway car, however, the fear is probably a lot more profound.

You may think I'm exaggerating or being ridiculous. I'm dead serious. I've watched skinny people slide by others in tight situations without the slightest hint of fear or concern. When a fat person attempts to slide by, or to be slid past, the fear is palpable. Maybe it's just general disgust, but I truly think that skinny people in Europe fear that a fat American will somehow contaminate them.

Of course in Europe, one can almost always choose a bicycle – that wonderful and glorious device that not only gets you from Point A to Point B, but also actually burns calories in the process. The main problem with bicycle transportation for fat people, as you may surmise, is the seat.

When I weighed 430 pounds, there was not a bike seat on the planet big enough for my rear. Unless someone found a way to mount a tractor seat on the bicycle, there was no way I could ride one – at least sitting down. Without getting into anatomic discussions that will make you squirm, the issue is two-fold: First, if you are skinny, imagine trying to ride a bike sitting on only the seat post. Well, that's what it's like for a fat person to try and sit on a normal bike seat.

Second, for men, there is also the issue of what to do to ensure certain parts of the reproductive anatomy aren't damaged beyond all repair. Bike shorts are designed to pad those intimate areas for both comfort and protection. Just try to find bike shorts that will fit a 60-inch waist without ripping wide open. Yep, not going to happen.

I dealt with these issues in two ways. First, I didn't start riding a bike regularly until I was below three hundred pounds. I made sure it had the largest seat I could find. I gradually downsized the seat as I downsized myself. Second, I would hop off the bike every few miles, in the beginning, and then every ten miles or so after I had lost a lot more weight. I never reached a point where I could stay on the bike for indefinite periods of time. Parts of my body that I did not want to go numb and fall asleep, ever, would do exactly that. It just became part of the bike riding routine and I'm happy to say it didn't stop me from participating in long distance rides, including a century ride (one hundred miles) that I completed in a single day in August 2010.

One of the true joys in my life that came about as a result of my weight loss was the ability to ride a bike again. There was still discomfort. My body will never position on a bike seat in a way that is truly comfortable. But like many of the challenges that exist because of being fat, I found workarounds. And I found great joy in zooming past guys half my size because my calf muscles were more than ready to propel my smaller body after holding up my heavier self for so many years!

I've had to deal with these travel and transportation challenges again in the interim years of trying to sustain weight loss and healthy living. It's discouraging when I realize my fear of flying is tied more to the size of the seat than it is the possibility of the plane falling out of the sky. And my bicycle went dormant when I passed three hundred pounds and once again found riding impossible.

But I haven't given up. My bike is sitting right in front of me in the corner of the room as I write this. It motivates me to make better choices so I can ride it like I did previously. I know it will happen. I haven't lost hope. One of the tricks to maintaining hope is finding ways to turn fears and frustrations into motivators to do better – one day, one step, one seat, one success at a time.

10

Baseball, Hot Dogs, Revival Meetings, and Heart Disease

I've already confessed my unhealthy infatuation with donuts. Infatuations often lead to obsessions and a person can quickly become strung out and dysfunctional as they seek to find their next experience with the object of their obsession. Such is the case for me with restaurants. I've rarely met a restaurant in which I wasn't interested in establishing a long-term love affair. The only restaurants that met my derision were ones with portions that were too small.

Of course, that automatically rules out every single restaurant in Europe, and probably most of the rest of the world for that matter. We Americans have somehow prided ourselves in making our restaurant portions bigger and better than anywhere else. Some restaurants actually market based on their obscene portions.

Is it any wonder that a visit to these places generally finds them well-populated with fat Americans? I was no exception. To this day, and probably every day for the rest of my life, I will find restaurant portion control to be one of the most difficult things to manage.

So, back to the disgustingly huge portion sizes. I'm not sure at what age I decided that normal was not enough. I'm old enough to remember the invention of the McDonald's combo meal, which in its early days cost $2.99. For that low price, you could get a Big Mac, a medium fry, and a large drink. Keep in mind that this was well before the "Super Size Me" phenomenon, so the medium fry was truly medium, and the large drink was twenty ounces. I blissfully ate many a No. 1 Combo because I have an affection for Big Macs.

Soon, McDonald's realized that Americans were getting fatter and wanted more food. At first, they offered the opportunity to add another Big Mac for a dollar. Thus, I could get two Big Macs, a medium fry and a large drink for $3.99! What I didn't care to know or realize at that time was that I had just upped my calorie count by more than 500 calories and added another 29 grams of fat to my arteries! At that point in history, nutrition facts were never on public display in a restaurant, and no one really cared or paid much attention anyhow.

Eventually, McDonald's figured out that Americans also like the idea of a bargain and that there were plenty of fat people or people ripe for becoming fat who would respond to the Super Size Me mantra. How incredibly ironic that Super Size Me at McDonald's really ended up "super sizing" a lot of people! Now, for only fifty cents more, you could have a large fry and a super-size drink, which meant thirty-two ounces of pop. An increase of roughly four hundred calories for only fifty cents? Who could pass that up?

It's not my intention to beat up on McDonald's. I'm not going to take the time or space to dive into the fast food wars. Documentaries such as *Super Size Me* revealed how marketing, profits and customer demand drove much of the growth in portion sizes at fast food places, which eventually poured over into sit-down establishments as well.

McDonald's is a corporation in a capitalist economy that was responding to market trends and consumer demands. We consumers willingly begged for what they were offering in ever-increasing amounts, and they obliged. I would like to give kudos to McDonald's for adding calorie counts to its menus and being more intentional about offering healthier options. I imagine their motivation once again comes from market pressure, but it's a step in the right direction. Good for them.

One of my favorite high school and early college days hangouts was a restaurant in St. Johns, Michigan, called The Wheel Inn. It was your ubiquitous 1950s style, 24-hour diner, located on Michigan's original north/south trunk line through the center of the state. During my first few years of college, I worked at a grocery store located just a short distance away. The grocery store was also a 24-hour operation, and my shift often ended at midnight or after.

My brother, also a night owl, and our friend Natalie, who worked at the same grocery store, would often meet me at "The Wheel" (as all the locals called it) after my shift ended. We spent many hours there, laughing, drinking coffee and pop, and loading up at the worst possible time of the day on some of The Wheel's most famous diner delicacies.

I loved their hot dogs. Hot dogs were one of my more frequent vices, or their closely related cousin, the polish sausage. I'd order two or three hot dogs, loaded with onions, pickles, and ketchup, a side of french fries, and the Wheel's best-known specialty, a homemade cinnamon roll as big as a baby's head sliced and grilled in butter and covered with at least a cup of the tastiest frosting in all of Michigan. Sometimes I'd ask for extra frosting on the side in which to dip my french fries.

The food and fellowship were delicious, and I don't really regret those times, even though my heart and health certainly suffered. It was at The Wheel Inn that I would first come to terms with owning my man boobs. Natalie's sister was visiting from out of town, and in the course of our conversation, I admitted for the first time that "I have exceptionally large breasts for a male." It just popped out and seemed pertinent in the moment. I have no recollection of what we were talking about that led to it seeming like an appropriate moment to self-disclose! But I was more comfortable talking about my man boobs after that. Ah, the memories.

Restaurants are a fat person's crack house. Perhaps nowhere is this truer than at the buffet. Buffets are brothels for fat people. After I lost 230 pounds and was forced to occasionally join my family at the local Ponderosa, I suddenly realized that the ratio of fat people was much higher than at most other restaurants. I had to work my way around the 600-pound man in a cart hooked up to oxygen who was making his way along the dessert line. A quick perusal of my surroundings revealed that nearly everyone in the room was significantly overweight or accompanying an overweight person.

Buffets make their money by selling cheap food by volume, meaning that large portions of cheap and unhealthy garbage make a lot more money than small portions of healthier choices. Thus, the fact that your buffet is being frequented by people who eat three times more than normal is irrelevant to the bottom line. The types of food mean the operator is likely to still make money no matter how much a customer eats.

In my college years, the Chinese food buffet began to grow in popularity in the United States. Is it any wonder? By that time, the entire nation had begun to grow as well, and Chinese buffets not only offered the welcome familiarity of the buffet brothel...they included MSG, and a fortune cookie at the end! Who could resist that?

My favorite Chinese buffet was in a building that looked like a former Toys R Us store behind the Lansing Mall and went by the wonderful name of "Buffet World." Its Chinese status was not necessarily known until entering the building, but that didn't matter. What fat person could possibly resist the idea of a world of buffets? The allure of what is contained within is irresistible. Add in the fact that the exterior of the building still had all the primary color pomp of a Toys R Us, and there was no hope for a fat person who drove by.

Buffet World was indeed an interesting place, for more reasons than one. I first went there with my friend Char who was about twenty-five years older than me and had lived a yo-yo diet existence throughout her life. She loved to tell me how she was super skinny when she graduated from high school, but she had a difficult marriage and ballooned to over three hundred pounds. She lost and gained weight repeatedly over the years, and being my friend meant she was unfortunately once again heavy.

We walked into Buffet World, me at 430 pounds, Char at 300 pounds, and the host looked right at us and said, "Ah...you need table." Booths weren't even considered since the only way that they would have worked would have been for both of us to sit on the same side and push the table all the way up against the back of the other side.

It's hard to figure out the thoughts of Chinese workers at a buffet since due to the language gap, but I'm quite certain that the owner was concerned at our frequent presence and viewed us as a possible profit loss. I believe that the most significant damage to their profits was probably caused by the amount of toilet paper we used during a visit (Chinese food had a certain "effect" on both of us) and the number of chairs I broke.

I was happy to introduce many more people in my life to the thrills and pleasures of Buffet World. My brother quickly became an addict, and to this day, struggles with Chinese Buffet Addiction. My friend Jared quickly joined me as a regular. That is, until he had an altercation with two nosy women.

You see, fat people, and especially fat people at a buffet, create a lot of curiosity. As I mentioned in an earlier chapter, I truly believe that some skinny people think that a fat person may explode at any moment and cover them with squishy fat cells. Others are curious about what the fat person will order, or how many times the fat person has been to the buffet, and what is on his/her plate. Frequent stares are the norm, often followed by hushed conversations with heads shaking or nodding in agreement over the poor decisions being made at that very moment by a fat person in a skinny person's presence.

One day, two older women came in and sat down shortly after Jared and I arrived. The stares were frequent, the nods and tongue clucks were frequent, and some of the conversation became audible. Words such as "fat," "sad," "poor," and "can you imagine" were overheard.

Jared, who has always had more chutzpah than I, waited until we left to address the concerns these two patrons clearly had over the presence of the two of us at Buffet World. As we walked out, he briefly stopped by their booth and said, "What's the matter grandmas? Haven't you ever seen a fat person eat at a buffet before?" The look on their faces was priceless. It's a rare moment when a fat person gets a one-up on a skinny person. One thing I will always appreciate about Jared is his willingness to speak his mind, even if it's just to address a minor injustice that fat people endure.

I had to break my buffet addiction during my weight loss experiences, and that's when I realized more strongly than ever how buffets are truly traps for fat people. The correlation to a crack house is not hyperbole, although most buffets do not have broken windows and burned out sections with unsafe for occupancy stickers. I would argue, however, that buffets truly are unsafe for occupancy by fat people.

Speaking of unsafe for occupancy, restaurants come with a set of hazards not related to the food. Watch the eyes of a fat person the next time they enter a restaurant where you are eating. I guarantee that when they approach the "Please Wait to be Seated" sign, there will be a look of fear and consternation on their face. Why? Restaurants have booths. For skinny people who don't know about this fear, here is a tutorial, which I call the Booth Visual Identification System.

First, and foremost, it is imperative to visually identify and guess to the best of your ability, the total width available at a booth. It may be helpful to use nearby visual references that are generally of a set length (such as the standard four-foot restaurant table). Visualize moving that table over to booth and seeing how it fits, from end to end. Ideally, at least five feet of total booth space is needed – slightly more than one side of the table.

Second, and perhaps most importantly, identify if the eating surface at the booth is mobile. Is it also a table, with a foot, that can easily be moved in any direction? Or is it bolted to the wall, or part of the booth architecture itself? This step is incredibly important. A mobile booth has possibilities. A stationary booth is likely to cause issues and should be avoided.

Third, check the entrance and exit point. Some booths have no barrier, whereas others may have a step, or may be designed in such a way that it's necessary to move past some type of barrier or blockage to access the seat. This is especially problematic if the booth is a stationary unit. Avoid these kinds of booths, as the potential for embarrassment is great.

Finally, assess your guests. Are you by yourself? If so, a mobile booth is definitely fine, because you can push the table all the way to the other side, if necessary. However, keep in mind that stationary booths still may cause significant problems, and should generally be avoided. If you have guests with you, assess their likely booth attributes. Are they skinny enough that table movement at a mobile booth would not pin them against the back of the booth? Would they be willing to sacrifice some table space for your fat? Do you have more than one guest? Carefully assess the space available if you must sit next to someone.

This process sounds tedious because it is. During my fat years, I routinely avoided this process altogether by simply asking for a table. That didn't always work, though, because tables weren't always available, and tables come with their own set of dangers.

Most skinny people have probably had the misfortune at some point in their life of being crammed into a booth with a fat person. Recall that experience (if you are skinny), and you will easily understand why the Booth Visual Identification system is necessary.

I have had the misfortune of encountering booth issues many times in my life. In fact, I was in my teens when I first developed and began using this system. There's nothing quite as difficult (or embarrassing), as trying to eat your Mega-Schlop breakfast, when your fat roll is taking up at least six inches of the table surface. Yes, that's right, when forced into a stationary booth situation, my only recourse was to unceremoniously lift my fat roll and set it on the table.

If the table's surface was too high, then the process took on a slightly different method, whereby I sucked in, jammed my fat roll UNDER the table, and set my man boobs on the table surface instead. Both the fat roll and the man boobs made access to the food difficult. If I had someone with me, my food area encroached on theirs because my plate had to sit in front of the fat roll or man boobs. Not a pleasant experience.

As I said, tables were generally the first choice during my fattest years. The danger with tables is found not in the table (usually), but in the chair. Many restaurants seem to specialize in finding chairs from the junk heap, or from a restaurant that has already been sued because of a chair breakage incident and is now auctioning off the rest of its crappy chairs.

Chair mayhem occurred during the same trip to New York City I described in a previous chapter. Our group had walked what seemed like a marathon (especially for Char, who had a weak bladder and threatened to pee her pants repeatedly if we didn't find a place to pee soon – which is always difficult in NYC) and were on our way back to the hotel from the Metropolitan Museum of Art. Looking for a restaurant, we settled on a New York diner in the heart of Manhattan. As is typical with these places, it was small, crowded, and had seating facilities of dubious quality.

A quick assessment made it clear that the three booths along the wall were NOT an option. Thankfully, there was a table that could accommodate the five of us at the rear of the place. Char was grateful because the bathroom was right next to it. She peed (much to her relief and the relief of everyone else), we sat down, and she joined us shortly after.

Char had been seated for only a moment, when calamity struck. As we all pleasantly perused our menus, there was suddenly a great commotion, and Char cried out unexpectedly. We all quickly threw our menus down on the table and saw Char sprawled on the floor, lying flat on her back with her legs in the air.

She was yelling "Praise the Lord!" (Char's method of cursing) and trying to get back up (not easy for a 300-pound person in their late fifties). Our friend Gwen, in her typical laconic manner, chuckled and said, "What are you doing down there, Char?" It was difficult not to laugh, but thankfully for Char, I had had enough chair breakage incidents myself to have some compassion and help her up.

I wish I had taken a picture of the chair and could publish it here. Both back legs were completely bent and were now perpendicular with the back of the chair. They had literally bent all the way to the edge of the seatback without breaking. I had had similar experiences, although I am quite sure that I only had one chair leg act in such a manner.

The diner owners were extremely distressed and most likely fearing a lawsuit. They gave Char her meal for free, provided a different (and sturdier) chair, and gave her some ice for the back of her head, which had whacked the floor in a most disconcerting fashion. This, my friends, is a typical chair breakage incident for a fat person.

There are other chair incidents that can be equally embarrassing that don't involve breakage. Sinkage can also be a concern. I found this out during a religious moment in my life that did not involve donuts. There's nothing quite like sensing that you are sinking downward while listening to a fire and brimstone preacher underneath a tent during a revival meeting.

The member churches of my father's denomination do not easily fit into one box. There is a wide variance in styles, beliefs, and practices among the churches. My father's church is fairly progressive. The closest "sister" church is decidedly non-progressive. Plain dress, conservative living, and a continual call to holy living are the harbingers of their message.

This group sponsored an outdoor tent revival meeting every summer. For those of you who have not been privy to a tent meeting, think of religious scenes from *Dr. Quinn, Little House on the Prairie,* or *Cold Mountain,* and you have the idea. I generally went forward to the altar at least once during these meetings to pray for forgiveness for being fat and to ask the Holy Spirit to keep me from eating so many donuts. Apparently, the Holy Spirit complied during the meeting itself, but left a donut-sized hole in my heart on the way home, where I stopped every year at the Quickie Mart in Hemlock (try wrapping your head around the name of that town and its role in my life) for donuts.

Anyhow, one particular year, it had been quite rainy leading up to the tent meeting. I arrived along with some others from our church. We exchanged greetings with our conservative brethren and sat down for the service. Things seemed fine, until about fifteen minutes into the meeting, when I began to feel rather unstable on my chair. I feared that a breakage was imminent, but since I was in the middle of a crowd underneath a tent, I didn't want to draw too much attention by standing up at that point to assess the situation.

Soon, I realized I was not experiencing breakage, I was instead experiencing sinkage. My chair was slowly sinking into the ground – which had been softened by the recent rains (or at least, that's what I blamed afterwards). I was unsure as to what to do.

My chair continued to slowly sink, and my legs began to stretch out in front of me as I sunk lower and lower. It was not lost on me at all that I was at a revival meeting, and I was quite literally sinking down "into the pit." Was God trying to tell me something? So many people had told me I was going to end up in hell because of my weight, and now, I was quite literally sinking down into the "miry clay," a frequent analogy in conservative Christian circles to how Christians can sink so easily in the world's traps.

Thankfully, I was rescued by prayer. How appropriate, yes? The minister called for a time of prayer, and as I checked to ensure that most eyes were closed, I stood up, pulled my chair out of the ground (by this time there were perhaps six inches or so of legs left above the ground), and moved it forward a few inches to fresh ground. I still didn't know what to do after prayer, though, because I knew that if I sat back down, the scenario would repeat itself.

Prayer rescued me once again. An altar call was given, and I rushed to the altar, convinced that God had revealed to me in a very tangible way the condition of my soul because of my weight. I wept and cried for forgiveness and begged the Holy Spirit to cleanse my heart of its evil bent toward sin and donuts. I laid out the lusts of my flesh before the Lord and promised that I would serve God for the rest of my life and would dedicate my life to service if freed from the bondage of donuts and cookies. Afterwards, I felt a sense of relief. Perhaps I had escaped hell for another night, or at least until I drove home past the Quickie Mart.

As if dealing with restaurants, buffets, booths, sinking down to hell, and breaking chairs were not difficult enough, I often encountered another food trap in the form of the concessions stand. I rarely attended movies, so that's not the concessions stand to which I'm referring. I love baseball, that great American pastime that's as much about stuffing your face with every unhealthy thing known to humankind as it is to hitting the ball and running the bases. When I lived in Michigan, I would occasionally purchase a set of season tickets for my dad and I to the local minor league team's games. I quickly figured out their food setup.

Like most baseball parks, the options included your traditional fare at multiple vending windows along the back of the stadium. Sprinkled throughout the rest of the park were a variety of specialty vendors. It was in this area, just behind the section where we usually sat, that the mega-Lug dog vendor lived. A mega-Lug dog was quite possibly the world's largest hot dog – about sixteen inches long and as fat as a kielbasa sausage.

Mega-Lugs were grilled on a hot, buttered griddle piled high with sautéed peppers and onions. Polish sausages of a similar girth were available, but I never got those. I made a beeline for the mega-Lug dog, usually no later than the third inning. I'd generally get the combo deal, which cost about fifteen bucks and included a mega-Lug piled high with onions and peppers, a bag of chips, and either a beer or a pop. After taking possession of my sinful sausage, I'd head over to the condiments area and load up with a quart or so of ketchup and mustard, and a fistful of napkins.

In the days when I was not monitoring my weight, I'd often get a second mega-Lug somewhere around the seventh inning stretch. In between, I might have ice cream, candy, Cracker Jack, or some other heart disease-inducing product. In the days when I WAS monitoring my weight, I'd limit myself to one mega-Lug and make sure I included extra exercise or reduced my other eating that day.

I hate to think of the amount of fat, number of calories, and amount of sodium in two mega-Lug combos. It's amazing I didn't drop dead on the spot. Here's the thing, though. Complete deprivation of things like a mega-Lug is generally not advisable. What I mean by that is that all of us, fat and skinny, need to be able to indulge periodically. It's part of living a joyful life, and our bodies can handle periodic indulgences without extensive damage.

So, my philosophy these days, as I think of a more wholistic approach to life is that allowing an occasional mega-Lug is a wonderful thing. Sure, eating that kind of food frequently is likely to lead to heart disease or other problems. I've learned that balance in my life means thinking clearly and concisely about what I've been eating, allowing occasional indulgences of foods I love, but being aware of trigger foods that it's best to work at eliminating completely because they trigger my binge behavior. In other words, figure out what works for you, and don't allow excuses or denial to cloud your judgement.

Photos

I was hesitant to include photos because I doubted anyone would really want to see photos of someone who is not a celebrity and is also fat and overweight. However, some of my reviewers specifically mentioned they thought photos would really provide another window into the struggle with weight that is the predominant theme throughout this book.

So, I'm putting a few photos here, near the middle. I would really love to include photos of the "Carland Hounds" (whom you've met by now if you didn't flip to the photo section right at the beginning) and others, but it becomes very difficult to get everyone's permission to put a picture of them in a published work.

I do hope these photos give you another glimpse into the life of a person who struggles with a serious weight problem, and maybe add some additional laughter to your day as well. Enjoy!

As you can see, I didn't waste any time getting started on growing that belly!

Between second and third grade. My last summer in "children's husky" clothing. Shopping for third grade was my transition to adult-sized clothing.

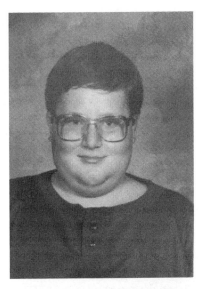

School photos. Top was fifth grade; bottom is senior photo.

These photos were taken about a year apart. I'm at my heaviest weight ever in both – around 430 pounds. I had a 62-inch waist (my waist was as big around as some people are tall) and wore a size 6X (XXXXXXL) shirt.

After losing 230 pounds, I rode my bike one hundred miles across northern Ohio in one day with my friend, Steve McKinney. I also completed two half-marathons.

With my future wife after riding our bikes in the Tour de Cure fundraiser for the American Diabetes Association.

Inspiring others with my friend, Jodi Davis. She helped me lose 230 pounds, and she continues to support me as I struggle to keep the weight off. BTW, she's kept off more than 160 pounds for fifteen years! My hero.

With Joy Bauer, nutrition expert for NBC's *Today*, before appearing with her and being inducted into her Joy Fit Club in 2009.

In 2009, I received the Charles T. Kuntzleman Award from the
Michigan Fitness Foundation and Michigan Governor Jennifer
Granholm for my efforts to inspire Michigan's citizens to live
healthy lives.

My wife and I moved to Florida in 2017. I've been working hard to lose the pounds that I've gained the last five years or so. Every day is a new day with new challenges, but I won't give up!

11

Does Skin Tone Come in Lobster?

I grew up in the upper Midwest, mostly in Michigan and northern Ohio, but also Iowa and Illinois. These locations all have three things in common. Cold. Snow. Ice. Some people enjoy these awful things. In fact, Michigan must have thought enough people enjoyed them that for many years the state's slogan was "Winter Wonderland." I had my own slogan – "Winter Hell." I hated cold weather and snow as a kid, and I hate it even more as an adult.

For this reason, I sought out warm climates for vacation destinations. Florida, where I now live, was always a top pick. I had family in Florida that were always willing to host me or pick me up at the airport. I enjoyed visiting with them and spending time in a place where my snot wouldn't freeze. Florida was generally a low-cost option as well.

In my early twenties, I decided to plan a trip to Florida with Jared and Lee. Lee was still living in Ohio (our friendship began when I lived there), so he drove up to Michigan to catch a plane with Jared and me. I was a little trepidatious about how the trip would go. While Jared and Lee knew each other, they had very different personalities. I expected there would be some interesting and hilarious moments.

As I recall, we stayed somewhere around Orlando because it was the cheapest airport to fly into, and being centrally located, we could drive to various places during our week there as well as enjoy Orlando's many theme parks. Shortly after landing, we took the shuttle to pick up our rental car. Lee, always focused on being frugal, had rented the cheapest car possible. The attendant drove up in a Toyota Tercel. For those of you not familiar with cars, the Tercel was Toyota's entry-level model. It came with four doors, but the entire vehicle wasn't much larger than a golf cart.

Jared is six foot five and at the time weighed about 325 pounds. His dad worked for GM. He looked at the Tercel suspiciously. Dropping his bags, he opened both back doors and began melodramatically trying to stuff himself into the back seat. He somehow managed to get in and promptly laid down across the seat with his head sticking out one door while his feet hung out the other. He looked at the attendant and said, "We're from Michigan. We need an American car that we fat Americans can fit in."

It was clear we would need to upgrade, and Lee wasn't happy about it because of the cost. I took Jared aside, and the two of us agreed to pay the additional cost. The attendant showed up with a Chevy Blazer SUV. Jared approved, Lee was excited about driving an SUV for the first time, and I was relieved everyone was happy. Disaster averted.

Other than Lee throwing up when he found Jared washing his feet in the bathroom sink (it really grossed him out for some reason), the rest of the week went fairly well, with one major exception. Toward the end of our trip, we decided to head over to the world-famous Daytona Beach. Lots of people recognize Daytona because of the Daytona 500, one of auto racing's premier events. The beach is also famous because it's one of the few beaches on which vehicles are allowed to drive. We looked forward to fun in the sun and getting to drive along the beach taking in the sights. Lee was the only authorized driver with the rental car agency, so he piloted the Blazer. We drove down onto the beach and made our way along for a mile or so before deciding to stop and get in the water. It was a beautiful, sunny day – just what you would expect in Florida.

We dove into the ocean and promptly began riding the waves. I've always enjoyed swimming, although truth be told, the ocean isn't one of my favorite places to swim because I don't like saltwater in my eyes and nose. But I wasn't paying attention to that today; I was just relishing in the warmth, sun, and fun that I was having riding the waves.

At some point, I realized I was a bit farther from shore than I intended, so I began swimming toward the beach attempting to catch a wave to help me along. After a few minutes, I realized I wasn't making forward progress. Hmm. Was I caught in a rip current? It appeared so.

I didn't panic initially, which is surprising. I began to swim sideways, parallel to the shore, which is what I recalled a person was supposed to do if they suspected being caught in a rip current. The main reason I didn't panic, however, was because Jared was nearby, perhaps ten feet away.

"Hey, are you still able to touch bottom," I shouted at Jared.

"Yeah, why?"

"It's over my head here, and I'm caught in a current. Come over here and grab ahold of my hand and pull me back in," I said.

Jared started to move toward me, but suddenly, we heard what sounded like an air raid siren. I looked toward shore and felt something or someone grab me. I momentarily freaked thinking that on top of my current troubles, I was now being viewed as a shark's dinner!

"We've got you sir," a voice said. "Grab this board."

Confused, I whirled around and found myself staring in the face of a member of the cast of Baywatch. I squinted, not being able to see much at all without my glasses and due to the saltwater in my eyes. David Hasselhoff, is that you?

I suddenly realized what was going on. The lifeguards had spotted me, sounded the alarm, and were now in the water performing a rescue. I was embarrassed. I told the lifeguard I just needed someone to push or pull me a bit back to where I could touch bottom again.

"No can do," he said. "Protocol is we gotta take you all the way to shore and check your vitals."

During this exchange, Jared had disappeared and made his way back toward shore, not wanting to be associated with the whale rescue taking place in front of him. I looked around for Lee but didn't spot him anywhere. I relented and grabbed the board.

For the next two to three minutes, the scene from Baywatch continued, and I was focal point. The buff lifeguards towed me, Shamu, toward shore. There was absolute silence from the 100,000 or so people on the beach, all of whom were watching me and my man boobs make our way to shore. I was mortified.

I saw a stretcher on the beach and tried to protest again, to no avail. I dutifully climbed on top of the stretcher, which promptly collapsed dropping me to the ground. OUCH! Now I did feel like I had some kind of injury.

"Get the heavy-duty stretcher," said David Hasselhoff, loudly enough for at least 20,000 of the 100,000 people to hear. I continued to be mortified.

136

Eventually, they managed to cram me in the back of the ambulance and started checking my vital signs while chastising me about paying more attention, how to escape a rip current, etc. I didn't bother trying to explain that I had already planned a rescue via Jared, who still didn't appear anywhere nearby. I was released and jumped out the back of the ambulance. Most people had returned to their beachy frolicking, thankfully. I slunk away trying to draw as little attention as possible.

Jared and Lee both suddenly appeared. They had been sitting on the front bumper of the ambulance while I was checked out. I was sullen and embarrassed. "Nothing like watching a whale beach itself," said Lee, laughing loudly. "Shut up," I said. I reached around and began itching my back, which I suddenly noticed was itching like crazy. Great. Looked like on top of making the evening news (which I did), I had also contracted a case of swimmer's itch.

"Let's get out of here," I said.

We walked back to the Blazer and decided to head back to the hotel to clean up. Lee put the Blazer in reverse, backed up, and the SUV slid into the soft sand to the side of the packed down portion of the beach meant for vehicles.

"Oops," he said, putting the gear selector in drive.

He gunned it, and we went nowhere. He gunned it again, and I looked out the back window to see a huge stream of sand flying out from the rear wheels.

"I think we're stuck," he said.

"Oh, great, this is just great," I said.

"Let me see if I can rock us out of this," he said.

Lee began the tried and true "get yourself out of a snowbank" method by rocking the SUV slowly back and forth between drive and reverse, trying to gain enough momentum to get out of the sand. It didn't seem to be working; I saw more and more sand flying behind the Blazer.

Suddenly, we heard a bunch of screaming and cussing. I stuck my head out the window and saw two young ladies in bikinis covered completely with sand, which stuck to them like glue thanks to copious amounts of tanning oil. They were not happy with us, and I feared we might soon have a fight on our hands if we didn't get out of there quickly.

I looked back toward the front and saw the four-wheel drive transfer case next to the gear shifter.

"Lee! This thing has four-wheel drive! Put it in four-wheel drive!!"

Lee complied, and the Blazer shot out of its self-inflicted sandpit onto the packed sand. We made a beeline for the exit.

I'd like to say that was the end of that really bad day, but several hours later, having showered and lathered myself in Gold Bond to try and combat the swimmer's itch, I felt feverish. I looked in the mirror and saw an extremely red face staring back at me. Yep, I had completely forgotten the sunscreen.

"Isn't that just a perfect end to this crappy day," I thought. "I look like a freaking lobster."

You would think that experience would have jogged my mind about the necessity of sunscreen prior to a particularly bad episode on Lake Michigan several years after the Daytona Beach beaching.

Lee had called me up and asked if I wanted to spend the Independence Day holiday in northern Michigan along the Lake Michigan shore. He was going to rent a speedboat and was planning an excursion following the Lake Michigan shore for several miles. It sounded like fun to me. I asked him who was going.

"You, me, mom, Twila, and I thought I'd see if Char and Nancy (Char's sister) want to go," he said.

"Will the boat be big enough?" I asked.

This question was usually the first thing to pop into my mind when I was asked to participate in any activity that involved limited space. I always assumed I would take up the space of at least two people, so it was important to know if the boat was big enough to accommodate my size.

"Yeah, they said it holds seven people, and we only have six. Plus, we're thinking of renting a jet ski, too. So, one or two people can ride that if they want," he said.

"Count me in," I said.

The holiday weekend approached. Lee, his mom, and Twila drove up from Ohio and spent the night with my family. Char and Nancy joined us early the next morning. On the way there, Lee told me our hotel was in Muskegon, but we'd be putting the boat in near Pentwater, several miles north of there. He planned to hug the coastline from there to Ludington, about thirty miles round trip. I asked him if he knew how to drive a boat.

"No, not really, but they said they'd teach me the controls before we left," he said.

My not-yet-fully-formed-pre-frontal cortex didn't compute the stupidity of someone who doesn't know how to drive a boat driving one on the open waters of Lake Michigan for thirty miles.

"Sounds great," I said.

We arrived in Pentwater and saw the rental company putting the boat and jet ski in the water. I walked over to the boat, surprised that it didn't look very big for supposedly holding up to seven people.

While Lee was learning about the controls, I walked around the boat and noticed a large sticker affixed to the side.

"Capacity: Seven persons or 800 pounds."

I did a doubletake. Math has never been my gift, but I quickly surmised that I weighed 430 pounds – more than half the allowed weight – and there were still five people to go. Next in my calculations, Char, who weighed in at about 260 pounds. We had 110 pounds left for four people.

"Um, excuse me sir. Should we be worried about the weight limit? There are only six of us, but as you can see, several of us are a bit larger than the average bear," I said timidly to the boat owner.

I'm sure my face was red from the embarrassment of being the one to address the weight issue and also being the fattest person present.

"Yeah, that sticker is so stupid," he said. "You guys might want to keep one of you heavy ones on the jet skis, but you should be fine." He left shortly thereafter, and we began climbing in, one by one. Twila, the next to smallest of our brood, made clear the jet ski was hers, and she was going to be the first to ride it.

The remaining fourteen hundred or so pounds of us found places to sit. Lee gently pushed the boat from the dock. I looked over the side and noticed the water was lapping at the small lip around the perimeter of the boat. In other words, the water was right up to the top edge of the boat. I felt an ominous foreboding. No one was willing to climb on the jet ski with Twila at that time, so Lee slowly maneuvered us through the channel toward Lake Michigan.

"This seems to be going OK," I thought.

The boat was moving slowly through the water and it seemed to rise a bit out of the water as we began to get underway. We approached the outlet to Lake Michigan. Lee, excited at the prospect of open water and his first foray as a captain, slammed the throttle all the way forward.

The boat leapt forward at a terrifying rate with the front seeming to come right up out of the water. I thought it might not stop and the boat would flip right over! Lee's mom screamed as she slid off the area near the bow where she had been sitting and tumbled toward the rear of the boat. Never one to have significant amounts of dexterity, it seemed like I was watching a slow-motion reel of the end of her life as she slid toward the engines at the back. I grabbed, we all grabbed, and somehow managed to keep her in the boat.

"Slow down!!" I screamed at Lee. He turned around, saw the terrified looks on our faces, and backed off the throttle. The boat settled into the waves. We all promptly grabbed our lifejackets, which were not required, but now seemed like a wise thing to wear. I made sure Lee's mom was safely secured in hers and that she was sitting in a more stable part of the boat. I should have seen her near death as an omen of what was yet to come, but I settled back down, confident that all would be well. I was so, so, so mistaken.

Shortly after the mother almost overboard incident, Nancy spoke up. "I have to pee," she said. Lee looked at her, then looked at me.

"What?" I said. "Why are you looking at me?"

"I guess I didn't think about needing to pee while we're in the boat," Lee said. "I figured we would just go in the water when we took breaks."

"I'm not planning to pee in Lake Michigan," Nancy said. "You'll have to find somewhere to stop."

We began scouring the coastline, looking for a marina, state park, or someplace we could stop the boat. All we saw were pine trees.

"I have to pee, too," said Char.

Praise be – a sign for a marina appeared before us. Lee steered the boat toward the shore, but we quickly discovered that the marina was designed for yachts, not small, overloaded powerboats. The dock loomed several feet above us in the air.

"Oh, look," I said. "There's a ladder coming down to the water over there."

Lee maneuvered the boat toward the ladder, which upon further inspection, proved to be made of narrow slats nailed to the dock posts. It appeared to be of dubious quality, but we had no choice. By this time, I had to pee, too.

One by one, we gingerly stepped from the boat to the rickety ladder. Lee and I took turns behind the older ladies, helping push them toward the top and steadying them as they made their way up the rickety ladder.

Then it was my turn. Would it hold? I stepped on the bottom rung and prayed to God to let the ladder hold long enough for me to get to the top. This is just one example of the nearly constant anxiety that goes along with being extremely fat. I never knew when I might encounter something that could not handle my weight, leaving me behind or in distress, or both. Thankfully, the ladder held. We all did our business and then gingerly worked our way back down to the boat.

We headed back into the open water. Lee decided he wanted to use the jet ski, so I took his place at the boat controls. We had no idea where we were going, but kept the shore in sight, thinking Ludington would arrive before us soon. As time passed, cliffs began looming over us, and we found ourselves feeling increasingly isolated. Everyone was getting tired and cranky, so Lee, who had returned to captain the boat, turned toward what looked like a small beach and attempted to "beach" the boat.

SCRAPE...

That didn't sound good. I suddenly noticed the motor making a strange noise. I looked back and realized the rope that was tied to the innertube we were dragging behind us had gotten caught in the propeller. Lee killed the motor.

At this point, everyone was complaining. We were hot, tired, thirsty (we only had limited water on board) and burned to a crisp. I wasn't the only one who hadn't thought about sunscreen, and we had literally been baking for at least three hours in the hot July sun.

Lee and Twila worked to get the rope out of the boat motor. We took a brief rest and once the rope had been cleared and the innertube had been added as "person number seven" in the boat, we headed back out into the open water.

Twila and Lee were tired of the jet ski by this point, so I agreed to ride it. The only problem was I had to figure out how to get on it from a boat bobbing in the waves of Lake Michigan. I looked fearfully over the side of the boat. It takes quite a bit of alacrity to balance 430 pounds, and I knew there was no way I was going to be able to get on that jet ski in the open water. Thankfully, we were close enough to shore that I was able to touch bottom. So, I dragged the jet ski toward shore until it was in shallow enough water for me to get on it, and we all turned back to the south, giving up on Ludington.

Twila and Lee were tired and cranky, and Twila finally decided she wanted to get on the jet ski with me to get away from her brother. I brought the jet ski alongside the boat, and she attempted to get on. Losing her balance at the last minute, she grabbed the jet ski, and it almost flipped, but I quickly threw my weight in the opposite direction to right the ship. However, in the midst of the melee, I watched in horror as my glasses slid off my face and into the depths of Lake Michigan. Yet another disaster for a disastrous day.

I had not planned to be on the jet ski at all, so I didn't bring a strap to hold my glasses on my face during high speed boating or skiing. This was a grave error on my part. My glasses had now found their permanent grave, although I consoled myself by thinking how interesting it would be if they were found petrified in a layer of rock 100,000 years from now.

My musings quickly turned to fear as I became aware of the current situation. We were several miles from where we had started, and there was no visible shoreline or location for me to climb back into the boat. I had already determined earlier that I lacked the gymnastic skills necessary to climb from the boat to the jet ski in the open water, so I knew it wouldn't be possible to go in the opposite direction either. I was going to have to drive the jet ski back, and without glasses, I was driving blind. Well, maybe not blind, but pretty close as I am extremely nearsighted.

Twila tried again to get on the jet ski with me and was successful on the second attempt. She would be my guide to make sure I didn't run into anything. Believe it or not, our party managed to make it back to where we had started, although no one was speaking to anyone else.

Nancy drove me to Grand Rapids to a one-hour eye place so I could get new glasses. In the meantime, Lee returned the boat to a disgruntled owner who noticed some damage to the propeller from the rope incident. Lee somehow managed to convince the owner the damage wasn't from anything we had done, as he hadn't seen any damage directly from the rope. We all breathed a sigh of relief when the owner agreed not to charge us a huge amount to repair it.

Nancy, Char, and I got back from Grand Rapids around dark. Everyone was totally exhausted and headed for their rooms. I climbed in bed and fell asleep immediately. Sometime in the middle of the night, I woke up, shivering uncontrollably. Lee was in the bathroom also shaking like crazy.

"What's up? Are we sick?" he said.

I looked at him and then turned toward the mirror. Two of the reddest heads I've ever seen in my life reflected from the mirror with the whites of our eyes very prominent amidst all the red.

"Dude, I have never had a sunburn this bad," I said. "I bet our skin isn't regulating our temperature because it's so damaged. Turn off the A/C!" The next morning, we were greeted by several more red faces. I had peeled a whole layer of skin that looked like a face mask from my face that morning. Everyone was grumpy and felt like garbage.

"We all look like a bunch of freaking lobsters," I said, a point to which the waitress would readily agree upon seeing us a few minutes later.

"I'm already scattering flakes," said Char. She would continue to shed for several weeks afterwards, leaving a trail of flakes wherever she went. They would pile up on the red carpet at our church wherever she sat, and we all started calling her Pigpen as she had a cloud that followed her everywhere.

"I guess I need to reevaluate what I think about sunscreen," I thought. "I don't think skin tone is supposed to come in lobster."

PART 2

You'll Cry

"Those who do not weep do not see."
— Victor Hugo, *Les Miserables*

12

Gym Class and Other Terrifying School Experiences

School is generally not a happy place for fat people. This was especially true in the 1980s when I was in elementary and middle school. The widening of America had not yet taken place, so I was an oddity. My size was my most notable oddity, but not the only thing that marked me as different. I was also a nerd.

Today, nerds are considered hot. In the 1980s, nerds were considered fodder for bullies and jocks. I was also the preacher's kid (PK). PKs are subject to additional suspicion and scrutiny. Apparently, everyone loves the moment when the PK sins. Such moments present the opportunity to verbally assail the PK for his shortcomings, threaten to tell his parents, and find great satisfaction. There also seemed to be a sense of relief when the PK messed up. If the PK can fall from grace and not immediately be struck by lightning, God must extend some kind of holy permission to all who screw up.

I recall being teased about my weight as early as the first grade. Despite the best efforts of helicopter parents, which my parents were not, being teased is part of life and part of growing up. Every kid is teased about something and most find a way to deal with it. It's part of the thickening of our skin that is ultimately necessary to become a psychologically balanced individual.

Please don't misunderstand me. There is a difference between being teased and being bullied. I am qualified to make that statement. I put up with teasing every single school day for at least ten years. The teasing finally relented when I got to high school. I also endured bullying, but on a less frequent basis.

So, how do young elementary students tease a fat person? They mostly use words.

"Hey fatty!"

"Hey chubs!"

"Look out! He's going to sit on you."

Occasionally, the verbally precocious would chime in with something even worse involving a derogatory King James Version biblical term for a donkey.

I told my first-grade self that sticks and stones may break my bones, but words will never hurt me. I'd like to know who came up with such a horrible saying. And why haven't adults figured out that this phrase is an awful reflection of a verbally violent culture and put an end to it? Words do hurt. They hurt this vulnerable, overweight child, maybe more than some other forms of abuse.

I am sensitive. As a kid, being sensitive meant that I took just about every word that I heard literally. Imagine hearing that you are fat, ugly, and inferior multiple times every day, and actually believing it. Is anyone surprised that I am just a bit psychologically warped?

For some kids, school is a safe haven from turbulent and difficult situations at home. I had no safe haven. As an adult who has been through quite a bit of self-reflection and therapy, I can see now how my choice not to fight back in some fashion was probably not the best one. In my own defense, I wasn't taught to fight back. In fact, my family emphasized NOT fighting back.

Not fighting back - to the extreme - was almost an art form in my family. A significant part of our reticence was because our church taught that fighting back wasn't proper for Christians. Instead, we were supposed to negotiate and work through our differences. As a child not trained in the art of negotiation, I learned to be passive in the hopes that my nemeses would eventually grow bored and leave me alone.

It's been so long ago now that names escape me, with a few notable exceptions. Even for a kid who was teased and bullied pretty much constantly from the age of seven to fourteen, James and Jessica Smith hold a special place in my memory. They are memorable because what they subjected me to was pretty awful and because their abuse lasted for quite a while.

Shortly after we moved to Ohio when I was nine years old, I encountered the Smiths. We lived in a rough neighborhood. I rode a rough bus. It was quite a wake-up call after life on the prairie in a cornfield town in Iowa. Canton was rough, gritty (literally, thanks to the ash from the local steel mill), and at times, violent.

Our family was viewed with some suspicion because we lived in "the house on the hill." My dad's church had recently built a new parsonage on top of a hill with a huge yard. Our house stood out among homes that were smaller, older, and in some cases, even had dirt floors. Our house looked like a mansion replete with white pillars on the front.

As a result, most of the kids assumed we were rich, even though we were not. We were also white in an ethnically diverse area. Although there were plenty of other white people around, we were probably the "whitest" in terms of our lack of knowledge about other races, cultures, and life in the hood in general.

Soon after my first day of school, James Smith was after me. He had occasional help from his sister, Jessica, who was an eight-year-old version of Tyler Perry's Madea, except with uniformly bad intentions. Jessica was probably only slightly more than three feet tall, but her mouth took up more than half of her face, and she knew how to use it. The bus was one of the noisiest places on the planet, but you could always hear Jessica Smith's voice no matter how loud the other conversations were. Not only was she loud, she was mean. So was James.

I didn't know it at the time, but James and Jessica had an interesting home life. It seemed to be common knowledge, though I never verified it, that drugs, alcohol, violence, and generally unstable conditions were part of their everyday existence. They also had an older brother who had been to jail for stabbing someone or committing some violent act with a knife or a gun. He rode our bus, too. Yes, we had at least one violent felon on our bus. I'm quite certain he wasn't the only one.

James began teasing me with the normal methods that I was used to. "Hey fatty, hey chubs, blah, blah..." I tried to ignore him and just pray for him since I was reminded daily that is what Jesus would do. Jesus, as he was portrayed to me then, would also apparently keep his mouth shut and take whatever abuse James was dishing out. In my warped worldview, the fact that I had a savior who hung on the cross and took the sins of the world on his shoulders, meant that my shoulders should be able to carry the weight of some verbal abuse.

James' taunts eventually became more physical, and he started shoving me around, punching me in the back of the head, holding me down along with some of his thug friends, and passing gas in my face – you know, all of those crazy rite of passage things that boys do. That's what I told myself. I continued to pray for him, and after the bullying and physical abuse had subsided, I asked him if he wanted to come to Sunday School. He responded by kicking me in the place that hurts a man (and a boy) the most.

Much of this abuse happened on the school bus. Even though the bus driver observed some of what was going on, she decided that I would likely be a calming influence on James and assigned him to sit with me. That's when he began stealing my lunch money, forcing me to do his homework, and trying to get me to touch him in inappropriate ways. I was terrified, because if I didn't comply, he threatened to do all sorts of other horrible things. Based on what I had observed, I believed he would follow through on his threats.

During this year or more of hell, I tried more than once to reach out to important adults in my life. I began with the bus driver by filing a complaint with her about the seating arrangement. She looked at me, told me to shut up and sit down, and slammed the door.

Next, I approached my teacher, who looked at me, and told me to shut up and sit down. I then tried the principal – a highly frazzled individual who was trying to deal with recent budget cuts that had resulted in four elementary schools being shoved into one former junior high building. The result was a hugely overcrowded building, classrooms of thirty-five kids, and a lot of racial unrest due to widely varying demographics in the district. He looked at me, told me to talk to my teacher and the bus driver, and then went back to addressing a real crisis.

Finally, I tried talking to my parents. Talking to my parents was a difficult experience. First, it was hard to find time when both were available. My dad worked full-time as a pastor and full-time at a grocery store. My mom worked full-time at a nursing home. When they weren't working for money or for God's Kingdom, they were trying to keep up with my older siblings' sports and extra-curricular activities.

I can't recall now exactly how my discussion with them went. I suspect that it probably took place separately, and probably began with my mom, whom I usually saw in the morning before getting on the bus. My mom's initial response was, "sit down, and deal with it." Where had I heard that before? After I complained about James again, she thought for a moment, and then asked me, "What would Jesus do?" I knew that Jesus would shut up, sit down, and deal with it. At least that's what I had been taught to believe Jesus would do.

There was this strange conflict welling up inside of me. I had been taught to act like Jesus, which, in my church's teaching, meant setting yourself aside completely, and reacting to every situation with grace, mercy, helpfulness, self-sacrifice, and peace. What I felt welling up inside of me when James would come after me was nothing like those things.

I wanted to hurt him. I secretly thought that maybe I could. He was smaller and kind of scrawny, but I also knew he was strong because he had nearly broken my fingers on more than one occasion. I did have mass on my side. If all else failed, I could kick him where it hurts, and sit on him. I was pretty sure that would cause some damage.

At some point, I talked to my dad. I'm pretty sure his response was very similar to my mom's. They were generally on the same be-like-Jesus page. Eventually, I prayed, asked God to help me, and decided the best method I had available was to try and win

James over to my side. I set about trying to bring my tormentor to Jesus.

My compassion was fueled by two things: a desire to not have to deal with daily verbal and physical abuse, and a desire to keep myself and James from hell. Eventually, my methods met with some success. By the time he went to jail in junior high, James had pretty much started leaving me alone.

The James Smith saga explains perfectly one of the reasons for my weight problem. I suspect that many others who are one hundred pounds or more overweight and have been fat their entire lives may have had a similar experience. The major factor in a lifelong battle with extreme obesity is extreme self-hatred, and a good bully and regular abuse can foster that self-loathing. It's impossible to abuse your body to the point of near death without actually wanting to die. Of course, this desire to die is not readily apparent in your conscious thoughts. That's the sinister nature of it. It resides deep within and drives you toward death without you even being consciously aware of it.

My experience with James reflects how over time, I learned to NOT value myself in any way. I was worthless. I had no value. Adults, including important adults, basically wanted me to sit down, shut up, be quiet, and take the abuse. On top of that, I took on the responsibility for being like Jesus and the responsibility for saving the souls of those who tormented me. What about me? Was I just some sacrificial lamb whose destiny it was to suffer abuse for the betterment of a sociopath riding my school bus? Apparently so.

The teasing and bullying from the Smiths, and many others, were only one part of my school nightmare. Part two belongs to gym class. Many people have an embarrassing story to tell from gym at some point in their life. Try facing gym class knowing that every single class was likely to be terrifying or embarrassing!

Physical education now seems to be one of those things on the financial chopping block. This is evident in multiple ways, including the out-of-control childhood obesity epidemic. My nieces and nephews have no idea what it was like back in the day when gym class alternated between two days one week, and three days the next.

I don't recall a whole lot about gym class in elementary school. I do remember playing the parachute game, which was kind of fun. I also remember riding around on scooters. I sometimes was sidelined from scooters because I was so fat the wheels wouldn't roll, or they would dig into the gym floor. That meant I got to keep score while everyone else had fun zooming around the gym.

I do recall quite a bit about my gym class experiences in junior high. Junior high gym class meant graduating to required showers afterwards, jock straps, and a host of other painful experiences too numerous to list here. I recall many episodes of total and utter humiliation, in ways that now seem both tragic and funny.

My junior high gym teacher was Mr. Miller. I would like to think that we were related, since my mom's maiden name is Miller, but that's almost always a go-nowhere proposition, since Miller is one of the top ten surnames in the United States. Mr. Miller was also the high school baseball coach. He was tall, sturdy, and muscular. He wasn't overly mean, but he also didn't take any crap in the stereotypical male gym teacher kind of way.

I tried to make Mr. Miller feel sorry for me and my "situation." I quickly learned that was a useless endeavor. When especially egregious gym activities were scheduled, I would try to use the sick card. Sometimes that would work, especially when gym class was in the afternoon and I could pretend that I got sick from the cafeteria food. I suspect this may have worked better because Mr. Miller probably got sick just LOOKING at the cafeteria food. He was always eating some kind of fruit or vegetable that he didn't find in the cafeteria during the lunch hour.

Two experiences during these three years of gym hell stick out in my mind. First was the Presidential Physical Fitness Test, which was some sort of barbaric physical assessment tool developed by skinny people during the Kennedy Administration. This test was supposed to measure a student's physical fitness. It had a companion Presidential Academic Fitness Test that was supposed to measure your academic prowess, or lack thereof. I routinely failed the physical fitness test and scored off the charts on the academic assessment. Remember, I was a nerd. Fat nerds usually did well on the academic test. We took our kudos wherever they were available.

The Presidential Physical Fitness test included several different components designed to measure a person's physical condition. The only one that I ever came close to passing was the shot put. It's that whole mass and velocity thing that I mentioned earlier, because believe me, I did not have much upper body strength, nor did I practice the shot put or even pick up a shot put any other time of the year. Two other components are memorable because of the extreme trauma they induced.

The first was one that I like to think was traumatic for many young men. At least that's what I told myself when I observed that I was not the only one who struggled. It was the rope test. I think the Boy Scouts may terrorize their members with this test also.

Basically, you are supposed to climb as high as you can on a long, thick rope hung from the gym ceiling. It measures upper body strength. Makes sense, right? Well, the test was exceptionally easy for me to fail every year. All I could do was hang on the bottom of the rope for only a few seconds. Yes, surrounded by my classmates, I had the opportunity to publicly humiliate myself by walking up to the rope, grabbing the end, and then swinging there for a few moments like an ape swinging on a tree branch.

"Pull yourself up," Mr. Miller would say.

I would wince, grit my teeth, pull, and…move absolutely nowhere.

"Pull yourself up, Stanton…use your arms, and pull yourself up the rope."

I would grunt, wince, grit my teeth, and…yep, no motion. Nada. Perhaps I generated a bit of a swinging motion, but I was just hanging there, with absolutely no vertical motion at all.

"Zero," Mr. Miller would call out, publicly assigning a number to my failure.

By the time my third and final year with Mr. Miller came around, he didn't even bother making me try. I'd walk up to the rope, grab the end. While my feet were still on the floor, he'd look up and say, "Zero," and I'd go on my way to the next torturous endeavor.

The second humiliating component of the fitness test was the mile run. This was done outside on the school's track, the one used by extremely skinny people who wear shorts that are entirely too short and somehow manage to leap like gazelles over wooden blockades without breaking their necks or rendering themselves completely sterile for the rest of their lives.

As I recall, we had to run around the track four times to complete the mile. We all started together. I quickly moved to the rear of the pack. Well, actually, I didn't move to the rear; it's just that within twenty seconds or less, everyone else moved out in front of me. I was usually lapped within a couple of minutes, and then lapped again, and again…you get the idea. I always hoped Mr. Miller would get confused because I had been lapped so many times and would think I had gone around four times instead of three, but he must have kept his eye on me.

As the other boys finished the run, they headed over to the nearby baseball diamond and began playing baseball. I usually finished the run by the bottom of the sixth or seventh inning. Of course, I hadn't run for the past half hour. Running lasted about thirty seconds. The rest of the test, I was walking.

Not only could I not breathe when I ran, my fat would swing from side to side, making an unceremoniously loud slapping sound when I attempted to run. I suppose the rhythm of my fat could have been used to help set the pace or cadence, but since I was soon left completely by myself in a group of one assigned to the "one-hour pace" group, it was just an uncomfortable annoyance. So, I walked. My one saving grace was that so long as I finished, Mr. Miller gave me credit, which helped me get at least a few points.

The other wonderful gym experience during this era involved playing basketball either half-naked or jammed like sausage in a casing into some universal "one size fits all" (what a lie) jersey. I would gladly choose the sausage jersey over hearing Mr. Miller say, "Shirts vs. Skins."

That phrase would strike fear into the heart of anyone present with a man boob problem. "Oh, please God, please let me be on the Shirts; PLEASE, PLEASE, PLEASE let me be on the Shirts!" It always boiled down to fate. We would count off, "Shirt, Skin, Shirt, Skin" and I would make some futile attempt at shuffling to get in the right spot, but that didn't always work. Those days I landed on the Skins were some of the worst of my life. I would see my classmates recoil in horror as well. It wasn't pleasant for anyone in the vicinity.

If you've never experienced the humiliation yourself, you've probably surmised that "Skins" meant playing the game with no shirt. For most teenage boys, this is not an issue. For fat teenage boys, and especially fat teenage boys whose man boobs were bigger than many of the teenage girls on the other side of the bleachers, it was a nightmare.

I considered myself an okay basketball player. I could shoot baskets pretty well. As long as it was only a half-court game, I could move around quickly enough without gasping for air or passing out to actually contribute to my team. This was a matter of pride for me, because when you are a fat nerd, you look for every possible angle to try and be one of the cool, athletic guys.

All sense of pride was quickly lost when I landed on the Skins team. I told myself it was God's way of keeping me humble. It was also God's way of striking fear into the hearts of other players and onlookers. It's a good thing the girls were on the other side of the bleachers. They probably would have run out of the gym screaming, with weeping and gnashing of teeth at the sight of my man boobs coming down the court toward them.

Man boobs are interesting. Perhaps interesting isn't the best word; terrifying, awful, horrendous, painful, or humiliating might be more appropriate. Maybe by using the word "interesting," some of the emotional burden is assuaged. I certainly can sympathize with the challenges well-endowed women face.

Playing basketball or any type of bouncy activity with man boobs is like seeing the opening scene of *Baywatch* go horribly, disastrously wrong. I'm confident there's not a human being on this planet who would feel anything other than terror at the sight of man boobs making their way down the basketball court or beach.

Man boobs bounce. They move side to side. They slap noisily against the skin. They basically cause mental and emotional anguish for all in their presence. If not managed carefully, man boobs may cause injury. Jumping too high to shoot a basket could result in taking a man-boob to the eye. A man-boob could leave a mark if you got too close during a side-to-side shuffle.

For the male with the man boobs, whiplash is a distinct possibility. The man boobs may still be heading west, when you've already turned to head east. I've yet to find a sports bra type device to support man boobs, although I did purchase a t-shirt from the Spanx company that helps a bit...but I digress.

The lesser of two evils when it came to basketball was wearing the sausage jersey, also known technically (from what I was able to surmise on Google) as a pinny. What a dumb name. Just sayin'.

Perhaps Mr. Miller was horrified enough by seeing my man boobs at work on the basketball court that he decided to spend some of his program's limited funds to buy these colored vests made from a netting material. A pinny is designed to quickly be slid over what we were wearing. This worked well and spared us (especially me) the humiliation of playing the game half naked.

Unfortunately, the "one size fits all" pinnies did not fit me. I had already learned that "all" really means "everyone except Jon." For the first year, I was able to slip my pinny over my head, pull it down, and then spend the rest of the day with a mesh imprint on my shirt or stomach because it dug into me so tightly. By my last year of junior high, that was no longer possible, and I had to simply wear my pinny loosely around my neck.

Surprisingly, despite all these challenges, I never received a grade lower than a B in gym class. I fought tooth and nail to get an A because I wanted straight A's. It's hard to put in words the pain that I experienced when I would get my report card and realize that I had missed straight A's and everything that came with it, such as the awards ceremony, the certificate, and the free pizza, all because of a B in gym class. I think Mr. Miller (God bless him) figured this out eventually and started giving me an A in gym. I remember my shock (and the shock of my parents) when I saw that coveted letter on my report card.

I decided to ask Mr. Miller about it. He looked at me and said, "You may be fat, but you give it a heck of a lot more effort than a lot of the skinny guys. Keep up the good work."

It was probably the one and only time during my youth that I received a compliment from someone in the athletic world. It also filled me with pride, but I quickly put that to rest, because pride is, of course, a surefire ticket to hell.

My school days included other horrifying experiences outside of gym class, too. Many days were packed with both humiliating and hilarious experiences. I could probably devote an entire book to just some of the things that happened to me during school because of being fat.

There was the time the desk-seat combo thing that I had to stuff myself into every day broke and I was trapped until enough strong people came along to pull me out; the time I broke the choir riser; the time I broke the piano bench while accompanying the choir (thankfully not the same year that I broke the riser); the many, many, many times I ripped my pants wide open along the seam between the legs, all the way from the belt loop in the back to the zipper in the front; the time myself and my other fat teammates broke the set of the popular public TV show,

Quizbusters (that was both humiliating and hilarious, for sure – they never put a team from our school on the top level again!); and the list goes on and on.

Suffice it to say, gym class and school weren't always safe places for me, but somehow, I survived and lived to tell the story another day.

13

Clothes

Covering your nakedness is a nightmare for fat people. In fact, it is probably one of the most significantly depressing and embarrassing parts of being fat. My clothing nightmare began about the time I was in third grade. I clearly recall my mother's frustration over clothing her rotund child. It all began at Easter.

Like most good Christian families, and our family was the best of the good since we were the PASTOR'S family, Easter meant new clothes. Our family was equilibrious: two girls, two boys, a dad and a mom. Unintentional gender equality thanks to the X or Y swimmer that happened to make it.

My mom has a knack at the sewing machine, so she would usually sew up the brightest of bright Easter dresses for herself and my sisters from the same material. Due to our church's strict teachings on attire at the time, these dresses were usually long, with frills placed strategically to eliminate any hint of female form. Think Amish schoolgirls with a bit of bling. In my much younger days, mom made sure to pick colors that would match her head covering. It was just as sinful to clash with your head covering as it was to not wear one at all.

My dad was destined to wear a suit since Easter was one of his more significant showings. During that era in churchdom, pastors wore suits and dad complied lest he be called before the church board for a disciplinary hearing. Until third grade, my brother and I wore cute little-man suits that matched my dad's and my mom would find color-conforming ties to clearly indicate that we were the pastor's offspring. To finalize our Easter Hallmark card appearance, the men of the family were festooned with boutonnieres; yellow if your mother was still alive, white if she was dead. It was a New England tradition that was part of my father's family traditions.

During third grade, my expanding belly finally surpassed the ability of underpaid garment workers to produce a child's size large enough to cover it. I had moved past "husky" and was officially in "men's" clothing. Perhaps I should have felt proud. Clearly, I was maturing at a much more rapid pace than my brother or others my age. Unfortunately, clothing manufacturers and America in general, don't measure your maturity by the size of your stomach.

My mother was aghast. What was to be done? The smallest available male suit for Easter was something like a 28-short with sleeves designed to fit a full-grown male, not a stubby-armed eight-year-old! Mom briefly considered working some sewing machine magic. She thought she might possibly be able to alter the suit down to my size.

However, she realized that if she chopped the pants down to a short enough length, they would have given bell-bottoms a run for their money. My stomach was huge, but my legs were your typical chubby eight-year old legs. In other words, they were about as wide around as a zucchini, not a full-grown male leg.

This dilemma began the first (that I recall) of the clothing lectures from my mother. Mom would wring her hands and pace back and forth in the kitchen expressing her concern that I was becoming so fat.

What was she going to do?

How was she going to clothe me?

Trying to get a word in edgewise was mostly useless in these scenarios. I would sit in the chair, feet dangling above the floor with my head hung low. I was causing my mother so much pain. I was putting our family's finances at risk. I was headed to hell. What was I going to do? Ah, I know what would make me feel better. I'd eat one of those cinnamon rolls on the counter, and maybe two or maybe three, if I could get away with it. Do you see a pattern here? This was only the beginning of using food as my primary source of comfort or consolation.

My mother finally decided that instead of suits, my brother and I would get matching Lacoste shirts that Easter. Yes, Lacoste, which was all the rage during the 1980s. For those of you fortunate enough not to recall that rage, Lacoste is the brand that embroiders the cute little alligator logo on the front of its polos.

Most of their designs of the era incorporated some kind of brightly colored horizontal stripes. Mom's plan was inspired by the fact that Lacoste fabric was so stretchy she could still cram my fat body into a 16-husky, while my brother easily made do with the size 10 or 12 (or whatever size he was – always smaller than what I was wearing).

Mom chose a bright red fabric with white stripes. As a result, I looked like Bob the Tomato with some sort of horrible skin disorder. My dad still wore a suit, but his tie matched our shirts. The happy family image was preserved. Unfortunately, my inner image took a beating, and that was only the beginning.

Clothing nightmares occurred every year from that point forward. I would develop stomach pain and diarrhea every August because I knew what was coming. Most kids look forward to back-to-school shopping; I dreaded it. My only joy was the rare moment when I could convince my mom to get the forty-eight- or sixty-four-count Crayola crayons instead of the standard twenty-four box. I cringed when it came time to shop for clothes.

Usually my brother was with us. I love my brother dearly, but during our growing up years, as with most siblings, the love wasn't always so obvious. My brother did not have a weight problem. He was skinny as a rail, good at baseball, and in no danger of hell. His back-to-school shopping experience was very different than mine. He is three years older than I, and by this time, he was able to select his own clothing. His only battles with my mother revolved around quality and quantity – not size.

My brother would head over to the normal section or wander off to one of the many normal stores for teenagers, while my mom and I would begin the foray into the adult men's section. Mom would start pulling shirts off the rack, looking at the size and price, and handing them to me to go try on. Most of these shirts looked like something from Mayberry, or if I was lucky, maybe something designed by Ocean Pacific.

They were all decidedly uncool. Today, unique style is often celebrated. During my era, my unique clothing was only a surefire recipe for derision. I was forced to wear what looked like "Grandpa" clothes to me because the cool clothes for younger kids simply would not fit me.

I seemed to increase one size each school year. As I rapidly approached adult XL, my mom became more frightened. Where was she going to find clothes for me if I outgrew an XL?

When it came to pants, I was fortunate and blessed that my mom knew how to sew. Otherwise, I'm sure she would have been even more stressed out because of the cost of alteration. I was also lucky that it was standard practice for my mom to shorten my dad's pants.

My dad and I have similar builds, which means we have tall torsos, and very short legs. Think of Mr. Spacely's wife from *The Jetsons*. Yep, that was us. I was only four feet tall, but I had a size 36 waist. You do the math, then the visual. Do you see the problem?

I would disappear into the dressing room (always wanting to disappear completely) and come out making my best effort to not trip and fall flat on my face because of the two feet of extra pant leg below my feet. My mom would get down on her knees and pull up the excess fabric, all the while telling me again that if I didn't stop eating, she didn't know what she was going to do. After all, our family was poor, and now she had to pay adult prices for my clothes. My weakness was a surefire recipe for disaster. Did I want to die before I was eighteen years old? I could have a heart attack at any minute!

Tears often would emerge during the back-to-school shopping. Now, as a grown man, I hate to admit that, but I was younger than ten! I was scared to death that I was going to end up dead or in hell or was causing my mom so much pain and suffering that I was sending her to an early grave. I must be a horrible, awful person. God must hate me.

If you grew up as a fat kid, I imagine that right now your head is bobbing up and down. Maybe your mom didn't know how to sew, and you had to face the embarrassment of wearing jeans with the extra fabric rolled up at the bottom. The only other fat kid in my elementary school suffered that fate. Maybe your family had even less money and you had to take what your parents could find at Goodwill. Maybe you weren't afraid of hell, but you, like me, were afraid of facing your peers every single day.

I know now that my mom's words were based on good intentions. My mom was overweight herself growing up, and that caused her to be more fearful. She knew what my life was like and what she had endured from family, friends, and the faith community because of her weight problem. One of my sisters also struggled with her weight and my mom's response to her was quite similar. Mom truly didn't know what to do, so, like most people, she did what she thought would change my behavior. I love my mom, and I know that she didn't intend to hurt me; it was just the nature of her concern coming out, and in my young mind, I didn't know how to interpret it as concern.

Issues with clothing continue to this very day. In fact, there has not been a single, solitary moment that clothing has not been an issue. Even at my lowest weight, I continued to have difficulty finding clothes that fit me well. A current or former fat man is never free of these nightmares.

A good example is the business suit. I have heard women remark that, "every man looks good in a suit." Whenever I hear that comment, I immediately add "except for me." It's kind of like the fortune cookie game where you add "in bed" or "on the toilet" at the end of all the fortunes, except it's not funny. When it comes to clothing, my fortune has been anything but encouraging.

I look like a gorilla or Donkey Kong in a suit. Until I was a full-grown adult, finding a suit or suit jacket that fit was impossible. On the occasions where one was absolutely necessary, my mom usually came to the rescue by making one specifically for my dimensions.

When I joined the high school marching band, there was no uniform in stock suitable to cover my girth. My mom and her sewing machine came to the rescue again. She would dutifully take one of the existing uniforms, find a material that matched, and go to work. Thank God for farm girl sewing skills! I was simply thrilled to realize I could march down the field without splitting open my pants.

That leads to another clothing nightmare for fat people – the pants split. There are plenty of mortifying things about clothing and obesity, but perhaps none is more feared than split pants. Every seam is carefully examined for wear and stretching. Underwear color is carefully considered in case there is an unexpected blowout. Preparation for "the split" may help mitigate the embarrassment – if you're lucky.

I can't tell you how many pairs of pants I split open in my life, because the number seems countless. The moment of spliture usually occurred when some type of acrobatic or contortionist movement was required to sit down (e.g. fitting in a restaurant booth, climbing up bleachers, sitting down in a low seat at a theater). Perhaps one of the most distressing aspects of spliture is that it could go unnoticed unless the surroundings were silent enough to hear the discrete "rip," or cold enough that you felt the breeze on your butt. I often had no idea that I had split my pants until they were around my legs in the bathroom. Once discovered, the cover-up operation began.

What to do, what to do… especially if at school with no easy escape! Again, it all goes back to preparation. I kept in mind a daily checklist in case of pant spliture:

Do not wear tighty whities. No one wants to see you in your underwear anyhow, so any thought of tighty whities being sexy is completely incorrect. They are a liability. In case of spliture, white glows in the dark and is much more noticeable than a darker shade.

Wear very long shirts. I generally bought "tall" shirts (along with big) not because I'm tall, but because if the shirt completely covered my butt, it served as a spliture buffer between my split pants and my underwear. Note: This feat was possible both with tucked in and untucked shirts. To be especially effective, consider shirts that are nearly the same color as your pants.

Keep a stash of safety pins accessible at all times. Some splits can be held together; it's rare, but sometimes possible.

Always have a back-up pair of pants in your locker, car, office, or somewhere that is quickly and easily accessible.

Practice the split-pants shuffle. Knowing how to quickly and effortlessly move from one location to the next with split pants is essential in case the first four steps do not rescue you. Strategic placement of arms or objects is an integral part of the shuffle. Practice it and know it well.

As if the humiliation of splitting pants wide open weren't enough, the ongoing humiliation of the shopping experience also continued as I graduated into specialty stores and sizes. America has an uncanny knack for denying its problems, often by using politically correct language. We aren't "fat," we are "clinically obese." We don't have to buy "oversized clothes," we get to shop in the "Big and Tall" section. The marketing guru who came up with that moniker deserves either a gold star or a lump of coal – depending on your perspective. I'm mostly in the coal camp. However, it was brilliant to lump together one of our culture's most abhorred traits with one of its most glorified to find some kind of equilibrium.

Ah, the wonderful Big and Tall section. My visits to this section of the store began when I was in sixth grade. With the widening of America, the sections and specialty stores became more prevalent.

The sizes also continued to increase exponentially. In the early days, 3X was about as big as you could hope for. I was constantly terrified about what I was going to do when I surpassed the 3X! By the time I did something about my weight, I was wearing a 6X and could order up to a 9X. For those of you who have never experienced obesity, a "9X" is a XXXXXXXXXL. There isn't room on the tag for more than three of those X's, so a brilliant marketer came up with just using a number before the "X."

The problem with Big and Tall sections in most major department stores was that they sucked, if they existed at all. They did NOT exist at the stores where all my friends bought their clothes. In fact, I never once bought anything to wear at a shopping mall. My trips to the mall generally focused on the latest "grease and slop" special from the food court, the electronics store where I could revel in my nerdiness, the book store where I could revel in my nerdiness even more, and if I was lucky... Spencer's, where I could pretend I was one of the cool kids or steal a glance at the inappropriate-for-a-Christian cards. Trips to the mall never involved clothing.

In my youth, clothing was purchased at Kmart or whatever discount chain was available. Wal-Mart didn't exist when I was a kid; can you believe it? Well, it existed, but was apparently still stuck in Arkansas. The problem with discount stores, as I briefly mentioned earlier, was the clothing was a throwback to another era. It was also made on a loom in Botswana by a person making two cents per hour, which also made me feel guilty. If it was a 3X, it would be a medium after the first wash. That's not the worker's fault, of course, it's just the reality of cheaply made clothing.

Luckily (please note the sarcasm), by the time I was an adult, America's widening had resulted in some new clothing options for fat people. I remember the thrill of walking into my very own specialty store, "Big and Tall – Casual Male" (which eventually became "Casual Male XL" which recently just became something else… darn those corporate mergers!) for the very first time. Wow, I could be Big and Tall and Casual? Who knew?

I quickly discovered two things: One, I was going to be paying for every extra square inch of that casualness, to the tune of sixty-dollar polo shirts and hundred-dollar pairs of pants. Two, these clothes actually lasted and did not shrink. Hence, I found that even though my wallet cried out in agony and despair after each visit, it was generally a better investment in the long run.

This store was a fat man's paradise. On its shelves, I found item after item of clothing that had actually been designed within the Common Era. I could dress relatively stylishly, and best of all, my former fears of spliture were largely alleviated because the clothes fit, and the quality of the looms in their region of China were apparently better than those in Botswana, although I'm sure the pay and working conditions were just as atrocious. I quickly signed up for the credit card, the reward card, and walked out with my bag loaded with as much as I could afford. I had found a store with me in mind. It was a liberating experience.

Thankfully, Jared also required Big and Tall clothing at that time, and he would accompany me to Casual Male XL and to a discount store we found that carried a lot of outcast Big and Tall clothes – Value City. Jared pronounced the "C" like an "S," and to this day, I have to remind myself not to do that when relaying any stories about our excursions there. It was indeed in a "crappy" part of Lansing and often looked like it had been hit by a tornado.

I think a lot of their clothing came from loom errors at the factories producing clothing for the specialty stores. I was shocked to find Ralph Lauren, Christian Dior, and other fancy designers making clothes for fat people only to have it show up at Value City. Marked with tags that said "irregular," the irony of that tag was not lost on the big and tall shoppers like me, who qualified as irregular due to our size. The tag was additional confirmation we were in the right place.

I was glad to have Jared along because I didn't trust my fashion sense, which has always been completely nonexistent. Being color blind doesn't help either. Jared kept up on the latest trends, or at least the trends closest to the latest trends that could be found in a Big and Tall section or a discount, clothing-outcasts retailer.

Shopping with him was an interesting experience. Impatient and always in a hurry, he would rush through the racks like a Tasmanian devil looking for something that was at least close to a current fashion trend. He would grab shirts, hold them up to the light, and if they didn't pass muster for whatever unknown reason, he would usually throw it on the floor. I'm sure the employees at Value City cringed every time they saw us enter the store.

"This is only a 2X!!!" Jared shouted. "Come over here immediately, Jon Stanton. I'm going to cram your fat rear end into this shirt if it's the last thing I do!"

Jared seemed to become enraged when the shirt he thought was perfect for him or for me wasn't available in our size. This was a chronic issue at Value City because not only were many of the "irregulars" unique, the store had no standard system for where they put things. So, you might find the 2X version of a shirt on a rack at the front, while the 4X version hung out several racks away.

Jared had no patience for such ambiguity. At some point, we were thrown out of Value City after he threw too many shirts on the floor and told the manager their clothing-filing-system sucked. I was relieved that Jared would no longer have to experience such anxiety and that I wouldn't have to deal with the fear of being mugged in the parking lot or shot while shopping.

A few years later, I became aware of the nation's largest online fat-man retailer, "The King Size Men Company." Their marketers, I fear, didn't quite get it. Perhaps they were all skinny graduates of an Ivy League school. They had nice items in their catalog, though, so I picked one up and soon realized the quality was comparable to Casual Male XL for lower prices. Plus, I could order online and avoid the sweat and effort of walking to real store.

The area where King Size Men received an F though, was that every single clothing tag was huge and prominent and said in bold, black letters "King Size Men Company." Was there supposed to be something exciting about the fact that I was a King Size Man? Human beings aren't akin to McDonald's; Super Sizing your human is not something to be celebrated or enjoyed like you received some kind of bonus.

I had discovered something about marketing to fat people and the fat people psyche. When it comes to clothes, just about every fat person experiences the same nightmare that I did. Marketers know that unless you cleverly cover up the fact that the person that you are marketing to is fat, they are probably only going to buy clothes when they absolutely must – which isn't good for business.

I can't speak for women, but I know that for guys, the only hope is to somehow encourage us that our bigness is part of our badness. "KING SIZE MEN" implies that bigger is better, right? I think some of their clothing items even included a crown as part of the logo. Or how about this one – "Big Dogs – wear your badness with pride." This clothing line at Casual Male XL has its own bad-boy label and usually produces the typical bad-boy shorts and t-shirts that are so popular among bad boys these days. In other words, be proud of your bigness and your badness.

I work in communications and marketing, so I understand these things. It's a sad truth, though, because in reality, the labels should probably say "Heart Attack Waiting to Happen" or "Joint Breakdown and Disease" or "Miserable Fatness." I've said it before, and I'll say it again; there is no pride in being as big as a bus. If anything, it's a humbling and humiliating experience.

Now that you are fully aware of what a fat person experiences with clothing, it might help you understand why people on *The Biggest Loser* and people in their families cry during their "reveals." I would wager a guess that virtually no fat person has EVER heard someone say, "you look nice," and actually believed it. Experiencing the joy of actually "looking nice" can be emotionally overwhelming.

While I was losing 230 pounds, I implemented a practice early on that I knew would be motivating for me. I would always keep a shirt or a pair of pants hanging in a prominent place in my closet that was one size too small. I would try it on occasionally. When it fit, I would cry, and then go out and buy the next size down.

I'll never forget the feeling I had when I finally reached "XL" and realized that instead of heading to Casual Male XL, or ordering something from King Size Men (or browsing the few big and tall items available at Goodwill – losing weight can be expensive!), I was going to go to the MALL and buy something from YOUNKERS – an experience I had NEVER had in my years on this earth.

I imagine the store personnel thought they had a crazy on their hands because I, a grown man, wept openly as I looked through the racks and picked out something that was a size XL and knew it would fit me. I had finally crossed over from the world of "Big and Tall" to the world of "Normal," and to a fat person – anything that is "Normal" is good and healing.

14

Skin and Other Bodily Changes

Losing 230 pounds has a remarkable effect on your body in more ways than one. You're probably saying, "Duh, Jon," but let me share some things that occurred when someone who has been extremely overweight for their entire life (or as long as he can recall) loses nearly half of his body weight.

First, your hormones go wacky, and that's true for both men and women. You may recall from high school biology that a person's weight and metabolism are controlled by hormones, mostly from the thyroid gland. If a person has spent their entire life being heavy and eating a certain way, those systems get used to it. It throws them into shock when things suddenly change. The upside, in my case, is that my energy levels increased rapidly.

The downside is that this same hormonal shock can affect many aspects of life in a negative way. For instance, I lost my hair. Before you laugh and say, "Well, you were getting older, Jon," allow me to be defensive and say that MANY people who experience radical weight loss lose their hair, including both men and women. I don't think it's a coincidence that I had a full head of hair until I started losing weight. Yes, it was thinning a little bit and I'm sure I would have experienced some additional recession. However, my head went through the global recession right along with everyone's 401(k) plans during 2008 and 2009.

Of course, losing my hair struck a blow to my already fragile ego. Well-meaning people kept telling me "bald guys are hot," but I had always had a sense of pride in my thick hair. It was one of the very few physical features that generated positive remarks, and now it was gone. In its wake, it left a slightly misshapen head. Depending on how short I decided to leave the remaining hair, I looked like someone from the Planet Romulac or a fuzzy butternut squash.

I also became a chronic insomniac. At first, I thought I just had too much energy to sleep. I welcomed the extra energy and the many tasks I was able to complete during the quiet night hours when the rest of the world was sleeping. My excitement was short-lived.

I soon began to experience some of the side effects of sleeplessness, such as an inability to stay awake at work, difficulty concentrating, and a desire to eat horrible food. I have read research articles about how lack of sleep affects hunger hormones. The impact is not positive for someone with a lifelong weight problem. I began to really struggle with staying away from junk food during those late-night hours.

Hormonally induced challenges aside, the damage to my ego from hair loss was nothing compared to the damage from my skin. Everywhere I went, my skin became a topic of discussion. It's interesting that one of the questions I was asked most frequently when speaking to groups was about the excess skin. People who are trying to lose weight seem legitimately concerned, even scared, about it. They should be concerned because it has an impact far beyond the possible physical complications.

In my circle of friends who have lost one hundred or more pounds, getting rid of excess skin gets mixed reviews. Roughly half have had their excess skin removed, while the other half either don't have a problem or have just accepted it as a lingering battle scar. I would have liked to accept the battle scar mentality, but my excess skin problem really caused me problems both physically and mentally.

When I weighed 430 pounds, I was big. Everything about me was big. People often addressed me as "Big Bad Jon." No one, including myself, realized that underneath all that fat, was a relatively scrawny guy. This was especially shocking for me because an excuse I often used for my weight problem was that I was big-boned. Well, I'm not. I also shrank, losing almost two inches of height, most likely because of less fat on my head and on my feet!

What was left behind in the wake of the weight loss was a person I didn't recognize, and sadly, I disliked even more. I tried to come to grips with this new person, but what erupted was tremendous insecurity about how I looked.

When I was huge, I stopped thinking about how I looked, for the most part. I learned to ignore the occasional stares and comments. I also learned to completely ignore my own feelings about how I looked and simply accepted that I was hugely fat, which meant I was ugly, and that was that, and there was no sense in thinking about it more. Case closed.

After I lost the weight, I knew there would be some excess skin. I kept hoping that enough workouts, enough ab routines, enough healthy eating, and enough everything else I tried would eventually get the skin to a point where it wasn't noticeable. It didn't happen, it hasn't happened, and short of extremely expensive surgery I have no way of being able to afford, it's probably not going to happen. Plus, at this point, I'd have to lose a lot of weight again.

What especially sucked was when I looked at myself as a thinner man, the self-loathing was much more profound because I didn't fit into any mold. To this day, I have muscular legs and huge quads, but enough flab at the top of my legs that it's impossible to find pants that look normal. That's impossible anyhow, because where my waist is supposed to be is what some who have been "blessed" enough to see it call my bread loaf; a huge, squishy mass of skin and subcutaneous fat that when not held in place by my pants or underwear, sags nearly halfway to my knees. This has remained, even after gaining back a lot of weight. I have to buy pants big enough to make it past the bread loaf to where my waist begins, which means the legs of my pants are always way too baggy.

When thinner, north of the bread loaf was a shockingly defined abdominal area. Yes, it was a bit flabby, but there was clearly a defined abdominal core. North of the abs was the most painful part for me to deal with; the remnants of some of the largest male breasts on the planet! Okay, before you start cringing from the TMI, just think of other big dudes you know, and you have to admit, man boobs come with the territory. Well, I not only had man boobs, I had MAN BOOBS, and after losing the weight, I had massive saggage left behind.

There are other distressing skin issues that arise during radical weight loss. Moisture collects around all that flab. It's gross, and if I'm not careful, it can be not only gross and smelly; it can also begin to break down and develop sores. Please note, if you are eating breakfast while reading this, you may wish to skip this paragraph and come back later. Oh whoops... I guess I should have put that statement at the beginning. Sorry.

The only way to avoid the moisture problem is to routinely use the "lift, wash, and wipe method" (LWWM). LWWM can be complicated, depending on the size of your shower, the size of your bath towel, and the beginning size of your body. Excess skin and flab hang, which means what's left of your stomach is now at your knees, and what's left of your man boobs are now at your navel. LWWM requires moving said tissue to its original location, while simultaneously washing the under girth vigorously with a washcloth and soap.

In the early days, I discovered it was sometimes easier to just lie down in the tub, lift the skin, rub the soap around, and let the water do its magic. This doesn't work in a shower stall, of course, and my primary bathroom at that time had only a shower. At least I had something to look forward to when traveling or visiting my parents.

Perhaps the most important component of LWWM occurs after exiting the shower. Getting those areas clean is one thing, but it's getting and keeping them DRY that is vital. With that in mind, I had to repeat the former movements, but now used a dry towel that I would leave in place under my skin roll while I finished taking care of other cleansing tasks. I'm sure you are thrilled to now be enlightened about my bodily cleansing habits, but since this is something I was asked about often, I figured readers might be curious.

Excess skin created other fun issues, especially during exercise. To lose 230 pounds, you exercise your butt off (literally and figuratively). This requires a tremendous amount of movement. For me, this movement consisted of walking at a high rate of speed, high-intensity aerobics, and cycling.

The extra skin impacted the walking and cycling the least but still caused problems. I have completed two half-marathons, and both were psychologically thrilling but physically torturous. I wasn't out of breath and my feet didn't hurt too much; it was my knees and my back that were killing me afterwards, thanks to the extra skin. Try to imagine walking 13.1 miles with a good-sized tire hanging on the front of your body. Your back and knees would hurt, too.

On the bike, the issue was mostly my breathing. To attain higher speeds, it's helpful to lean forward. If I leaned too far forward, the skin would press up against my diaphragm, and breathing became very difficult. It's important to be able to breathe when you're doing something such as riding your bike one hundred miles in a single day and during all the training rides necessary to prepare for that feat.

The other issue on the bike was more aesthetic: spandex bike shorts. I'm going to go out on a limb and guess that not many of the readers of this book are Lance Armstrong wannabes. Thus, you may not be aware of what is generally required to ride a bicycle one hundred miles in six hours.

Bike shorts are not optional. I don't care how small your butt is, being perched on a ridiculous excuse for a seat is going to require padding. Your butt needs it, and if you're male, other parts very much need it, too. For a former fat person, finding bike shorts that fit correctly and don't cause every woman and child to run screaming into the streets when they see you wearing them is very difficult.

For those of us who are middle age, saggy, or in my case, sporting a fifty-pound squishy bread loaf, bike shorts cause everyone, including me, to cover their eyes, weep, throw up, or some combination thereof. What the public sees is the huge roll of skin, suspended in time and space, by black spandex. It truly gives new meaning to the term "spare tire."

My issues with walking and cycling didn't come anywhere near my issues during aerobics, though. First, let me dispel a couple of non-skin related myths about aerobics. Yes, I was very concerned that people would question my masculinity because I enjoyed doing step aerobics. Thankfully, I eventually chose to not allow my enjoyment of aerobics to be impacted by what others might think.

Second, there are other dudes that do aerobics. OK, sure, maybe the only other consistent guy was the instructor's husband, but there were others who wandered in occasionally.

Third, it's completely ridiculous that more guys don't do aerobics. It burns a TON of calories and builds the muscles that are really hard to build by only lifting.

Fourth, if you're open, honest, fun, and make the ladies quickly realize that you're not there to ogle them while they're in motion (take a spot in the front row, if possible, to avoid this problem) – you'll meet a great group of gals who are fun to hang out with.

Okay, so back to how excess skin and aerobics do not mix. I participated in step aerobics in which we moved in a particular pattern (choreography) to hipster music. Some of these moves were fast and furious. Sweat was flying everywhere, calories were burning up like mad, and we all looked like whirling dervishes intent on a future career in a synchronized dance number in a Madonna video. That's a stretch, but I'm trying to build a word picture for you... so just run with it.

Step aerobics involved a tremendous amount of hopping, skipping, jumping, and rapidly bouncing back and forth between the stepper and the floor. Extra skin quickly became its own unit in the brigade, as it would often be doing its own thing rather than cooperating with the rest of my body. I would quickly jump

185

left, but my skin would still be hanging to the right, and by the time it caught up, I was jumping back to the right, while it was still heading left.

What occurred was a type of wicked whiplash, along with some very unceremonious smacking sounds as the skin made known its unhappiness at not being included in the overall motion of the rest of the body. Thankfully, aerobics does promote rapid weight loss. Doing aerobics twice per week helped me reach my lowest weight ever as an adult of 201 pounds. At that point, the excess skin was still there, but the fat behind it had disappeared to a level where the "swing, swang, swung" motion was no longer much of an issue.

Many of you are probably now wondering about surgery. America seems to have a fascination with skin removal surgery. Perhaps it's the closeted desires of those who are only slightly overweight to have a tummy tuck. Perhaps it's the "keeping up with the Jones'" problem. Maybe it's *Desperate Housewives* combined with *The Biggest Loser* and *Extreme Makeover: Weight Loss Edition*.

Personally, I believe there's some sense of revenge at work, too, because I have heard the nasty remarks people make when someone who has lost more than one hundred pounds mentions they had skin removal surgery. Somehow, skin removal surgery means they didn't really work for their weight loss. It means they had their fat cut off or sucked away. It's the same type of attitude that can arise when people find out someone had bariatric surgery.

Whatever the reason, people are curious, and I frequently get asked if I have had skin surgery. The answer is no. Usually that is followed with, "Would you have it now?" The answer as of this writing is still no because I've gained back more than one hundred pounds, and there's a lot more to my stomach again than just flabby skin. However, when I was one hundred pounds lighter, you can bet your life that I would have had skin surgery. In fact, I tried, but unfortunately, the roadblocks abounded.

As I mentioned, when you lose 230 pounds and look in the mirror, you don't know what you are looking at. My face at 200 pounds looks completely different than it does at 430 pounds. As for the rest of my body... well of course, it looked radically different also. At first, I was hopeful that my new body would finally mean acceptance and love from the rest of humanity – something I had craved my entire life. It was if I suddenly expected women to come crawling out of the woodwork after years of neglect to throw themselves at my feet and beg to be wooed by the new me.

This did not happen. I kept waiting. I dressed better. I started to lift weights to build more muscle behind the flab. Perhaps one of the most difficult things to deal with regarding extra skin is the fact that you KNOW you are extremely muscular because you can feel it and sense it, yet the world is clueless because your muscles are still covered by skin and flab.

I told myself physical attraction wasn't important. Except that it is. At least in the beginning. What else is there, especially in the online dating world where I had started to look for a girlfriend, to really catch someone's attention? Sure, I had one of the best crafted dating profiles because I'm a wordsmith, but how many women never even bothered to read the description because what they saw wasn't what they wanted?

My online dating experience confirmed what I already knew: The extra skin contributed to my unattractiveness. I knew that I wanted to have my extra skin removed. I also knew that plastic surgery is expensive, and that insurance companies work their hardest to avoid paying for it. I started a research project to figure out what I was going to do. I started by contacting my insurer, who promptly said, "It depends." That's the pat answer from insurers when subscribers call to ask about $30,000 procedures.

Thus began the long process of paperwork, doctors' visits, letters from doctors, and thoughts about how I could make my skin break down even more quickly, since skin breakdown issues or back pain seemed to be the things that would work in my favor with the insurance company. One person I met on Facebook, who had managed to have his surgery covered by his insurer, told me he strategically dropped small amounts of a particular fluid on areas of his skin to make the breakdown look especially bad. He suggested I try the same thing. I considered it, except I wasn't sure how I was going to locate what he was using. It's not exactly available on the shelf at Wal-Mart.

With that ball rolling, I started to visit a few local plastic surgeons. Plastic surgeons in Michigan do not look like plastic surgeons in Florida or on TV. Most of them make their bread and butter performing tummy tucks for women who have had multiple C-sections or quadruplets. They look like any other surgeon.

I had no idea what to expect, but quickly found that what I really needed was my own tummy tuck. It's fascinating to me that it's called a tummy tuck, as if they take the skin, and somehow tuck it under the rest of your skin kind of like tucking in a shirt. In truth they cut off the excess skin and sew the rest back together! I suppose a "tummy hack" or a "tummy cut" doesn't have the marketing appeal of a "tummy tuck," and I realized that good old American capitalism was alive and well when it comes to how to market having your skin chopped off.

I was somewhat encouraged after my first consultation with a surgeon, but also pretty scared, especially when he described the procedure, including breast relocation. This was something that I had not considered. I knew my chest was an issue, but in my extreme naivety, I figured the surgeon would hack off the bread loaf and pull the skin tight. This would eliminate the saggy boobs. Made sense to me.

It doesn't work that way. The surgeon explained that the tummy tuck (he also used some kind of "-otomy" to identify it) he did would be accomplished by slicing my skin all the way around my abdomen, thus eliminating the excess in my back as well. I hadn't even thought about my back. I couldn't see it in a mirror, so what did I care? He quickly pointed out that I would care very much if I had a flat tummy and a bulgy back.

Then he addressed my man boobs. My breasts have been an area of consternation for my entire life. I'm not sure when I first realized that mine were different than most guys, as in they were a lot bigger. I guess it was probably sometime in elementary school. Big man boobs run in my family. My dad has them, his dad had them, and I have them. Neither of them had them to the extent I did, because neither of them ever weighed 430 pounds. I never tried on a bra (despite weekly insinuations from my peers that I should), but I have no doubt that I was easily a C or D cup.

The surgeon explained that to fix my man boobs, he would need to slice all the way around them, remove excess tissues, then sew around them like a drawstring and pull the thread tight. Yes folks, he was talking about fixing my breasts using the same principle as a drawstring trash bag. It all seemed very unscientific.

I quickly learned something else about plastic surgeons, or at least this one. He was in it for the money. Plastic surgery is not a healing profession. It's a market-driven, make-big-bucks enterprise. I want to be careful to not paint all plastic surgeons with this brushstroke, especially since I did not feel that way about the second person that I visited. This guy was definitely in it for the money, though.

After the exam (a rather humiliating experience in and of itself, since you completely disrobe in a room where you are entirely surrounded by mirrors), he spent the next several minutes trying to convince me why I should completely ignore trying to pursue the insurance route and just plan to pay cash.

The second consultation was with the head of plastic surgery at the University of Michigan. This guy was nationally known, and the U of M teaching hospital is considered to be one of the best in the nation. My experience here was very different. The surgeon was compassionate and took time to explain all my options. Most interestingly, he disagreed with the "slice all the way around" method of the first guy, saying that almost always leaves noticeable scarring and unsightly lumps. Rather, he would do a cut only from hip to hip, and I had options when it came to my man boobs.

This doctor also performed the "drawstring method," but his recommendation in my case was to simply slice off my nipples, pull the skin tight, and sew my nipples back in an aesthetically pleasing location. This, he believed, would avoid the possibility that the drawstring might later let go, and require a follow-up procedure. The downside? The relocation method meant that I would lose all sensation in my nipples.

Many people laughed out loud when I told them about this option and my concern about losing sensation in my nipples. I admit, it does sound funny. I even smiled a bit as I was typing that line. Let's just say I had some concerns, and I'll leave it at that.

As it turns out, fate had a different plan. The second doctor also had staff dedicated to working with the insurance companies and had quite a successful record. They were honest and told me no insurer would cover the breast surgery. If I was lucky, and they pushed all the right buttons, the insurance company would probably pay for the tummy tuck. The surgeon told me I couldn't have one surgery without the other. If he made my stomach flat, but didn't touch my man boobs, I would look even more like Mr. Spacely's wife. Plus, no one wants to go through the healing process twice. It was best to do both at the same time.

My wife was with me (although she wasn't yet my wife), and we talked about the surgical and payment options on the way home. I was inclined to go with the relocation method because I wanted to look as normal as possible, especially with my shirt off. I had no idea how I was going to come up with the estimated $28,000 it would cost just to have my breasts done. We strategized, and we prayed.

A few weeks later, I received the first denial letter from the insurance company. I contacted the surgeon's office and was told I would receive several. They would pursue every avenue until they found the right street. Two weeks later, it was all for naught because my employer eliminated insurance coverage and instead gave a salary increase to cover the cost of purchasing an individual plan. Individual plans are not subject to the various requirements of group plans, which means nearly any procedure that is expensive is denied. The salary increase was only enough to purchase a basic plan. Even if the insurer did, by some miracle, cover the skin surgeries, I now had a $5,000 deductible to contend with as well.

So folks, there you have it. I hope this satisfies your curiosity about the process of skin removal surgery. Going through these experiences caused me extreme psychological distress. When I started to gain back weight, I told my wife I was convinced it was related to the excess skin still hanging on my body. She wanted to know why.

First, remember that most extremely obese people hate how they look and often hate several other aspects of themselves. They deal every day with chronic self-hatred. Second, even though it was HEALTH that initially motivated me to change and it was health that I continued to talk about, the longer I was thin, I realized that I not only wanted to be healthy, I wanted to be considered attractive.

When my expectations were not realized, I blamed the skin. This eventually led to false thinking and telling myself, "You look worse than you did before. At least when you were fat, you were proportional. Now you look like some misshapen freak." So began the road back into psychological and eventually physical destruction. It would take a few years and a large weight gain before I decided my physical health trumped anything else, and the journey began once again.

15

Job and Career

My first job was a summer stint detasseling corn for a hybrid seed company. This was one of very few jobs available to people under sixteen. Even though I lived in Iowa for three years, I had never heard about detasseling corn until after returning to live in Michigan. Many of my new friends were excited about the prospects for making some extra money. My friend Jared convinced me it would also be just flat-out fun.

I was dubious. I weighed close to three hundred pounds at the time, and it seemed apparent that this job would require miles and miles of walking in hot temperatures. I also wondered if I would be too wide for the rows of corn. The last thing I wanted to do was walk through the field sideways. That would get old really fast. I looked at Jared. I figured if he could do it, I surely could, so I signed up. It was an experience I will never forget.

Jared's sister Kristie rounded up the Carland Hounds. All six of us fit in Kristie's 1979 Oldsmobile Delta 98. The bumper nearly scraped the ground, but we fit. The seed farm was located about ten miles northwest of Carland. It was always an interesting ride. Somehow, we managed to squeeze three six-foot-plus McNeth's, one 300-pound wide-load (me), Raylene, Brandy, AND all our lunch coolers, coats, ponchos and other necessary accoutrements into that vehicle. Amazing.

For those of you who may not have grown up in an agricultural area, or otherwise have no idea why anyone would be detasseling the corn, allow me to explain. First, the tassel of the corn is the thing that pops up in the top of the plant as it approaches maturity. It kind of looks like a multi-pronged head of wheat. It might be helpful to your understanding to think of the tassel as a type of corn penis. As it grows and fills out, it becomes covered with the pollen, or reproductive bodies, that would typically fall off and fertilize the lusty ears of corn growing lower on the plant. The result is a corn cob is born.

Hybrid corn is a cross of two different varieties to create a third, new variety. For this to work, one variety must be castrated by yanking off its tassel, or penis. The castrated plant can then be pollinated only by the pollen of the other variety, resulting in a crossbreed, or hybrid.

The plants are planted in rows of three. The two outer rows are the rows that will be castrated creating female plants, while the middle row gets to keep its penis and serves as the male row. We would walk down the path between the rows with plants waiting to be castrated on both sides of us. I would establish a rhythm as I grabbed each tassel/penis and yanked it out, throwing it on the ground. It sounds rather barbaric, but even though scientists have supposedly found that plants scream, I never heard anything, and I have yanked off thousands of corn penises.

In a good day, we probably walked about ten miles through multiple fields. It sounds boring, except people like Jared made it fun. Jared was tall and he was a corn detasseling machine. He also set up a rhythm, usually based on the latest Madonna song that he was singing out loud and could chug his way through a row faster than anyone else.

194

Jared also instituted tassel wars. The tassels often had pointy ends and became the perfect dart to bean at someone a few rows over. Occasionally, a tassel would resist being removed and the whole plant would come out of the ground. After chastising the plant loudly for its cantankerousness, Jared turned those plants into missiles. I never knew when I might look up to see an incoming corn plant headed my way.

I worked at the seed farm for two summers. We were paid something like $3.85 per hour, since agricultural workers are not covered by minimum wage or workplace safety laws. It seemed like a lot of money to a kid who was used to living on ten bucks a week from mom and dad.

When I turned sixteen, I decided it was time to find a real job. Like many high school kids, I figured I would find work in a restaurant or grocery store. I began applying for jobs in the nearby towns and villages. Jobs were plentiful at the time. Michigan's economy was still booming, and there were four towns within easy driving distance.

Most of my friends were landing a job with only one or two applications. I had a few places in mind where I really wanted to work, so I began with those. I landed interviews but didn't land the job. Someone else would get hired, and then a few weeks later, it wasn't uncommon for me to see the help wanted sign again. I would go back in and mention my availability. Owners and managers would smile and thank me, and then hire someone else.

Sixteen became seventeen and I still had no job. My parents were not pleased with this development either. They were tired of my requests for cash to pay for various school-related activities or to go to the movies with my friends. I soon noticed yet another help wanted sign in the window of a local pizza shop. I had applied at least three times before, had interviewed twice, had friends who worked there who had gone to bat for me, but I thought I would try one more time.

I stopped in to talk to the manager. By this time, we had a bit of a relationship. Not only was she used to seeing me to inquire about a job, she was also used to seeing me two or three times a week ordering pizza or subs! I was concerned that I might appear desperate, but I simply told her again that I was a hard worker; my references would attest to that. She mentioned she had recently noticed I was writing articles for the local newspaper and commended me for my commitment to reporting on community events. I took that as a positive sign.

Apparently, the newspaper articles worked some magic. After more than a year of trying, I was finally hired. I ended up working in that shop for the rest of high school and came back to work there again for three years after a one-year stint away when I left the state to attend college. I formed a lifelong friendship with the manager, who eventually became the owner. My brother and sister both ended up working for her as well. She and her husband attended my wedding. Our families remain close.

So, what was the deal in the beginning?

Fat people are lazy.

Overcoming that stereotype is by far the most significant challenge for a fat person when it comes to a job and career. Other stereotypical difficulties are also likely, but the notion that fatness equals laziness is the most significant roadblock when it comes to landing a good job or having a successful career. Silly me – I thought my references, the fact that I was a straight-A student, the fact that I had worked in hard manual labor on a seed farm would prove otherwise.

My boss/friend revealed this to me after I had been working for about a year. By that time, it was apparent that I wasn't lazy. I was one of her best employees, and she told me that often. She knew she could count on me to work hard, pull my weight (how's that for an unintended pun?), and help out in a pinch. One afternoon as we were making pizza dough, I asked her why it had taken her so long to hire me.

"It was because you're fat," she said.

I was a bit taken aback, although by this point in my life, I had already experienced a number of weight discrimination obstacles.

"Really? Why would that make a difference?"

"Fat people are lazy. Why else would they be fat? You are not like many of the other fat people I know. You're not lazy. I was so worried when I hired you that you would be a lazy employee, but you proved me wrong!"

She smiled. "Oh, it wasn't just me, either. The other adult employees told me they were worried about the same thing. They also thought you would get in the way and cause problems by running into people."

I was suddenly aware of why I had not been hired at any of the other jobs I had applied for either. Fast food restaurants were likely also concerned I would get in the way. Have you ever observed what the work area of McDonald's looks like? It is a tight space with a lot of people moving around. Again, my track record, good references, and good academic performance... none of it mattered. Fat people are lazy and get in the way.

From that moment on, I knew I had a huge obstacle right in front of me, literally, that would negatively impact my employability and career options for the rest of my life. It didn't occur to me at that time that losing weight would remove that obstacle! Teenagers don't always think cognitively or see the cause/effect relationship very well.

The experience of finding it difficult to land a job early in life ended up being a bit of a hidden blessing. Like so many of the other experiences described in this book, I looked for a path around the weight-related obstacle. I considered my strengths and knew I was going to have to use those to their fullest extent since my appearance would always be a job inhibitor.

I knew one of my more significant strengths was my sociability. Once people knew me, talked to me, and spent some time with me – they usually warmed up to me. I was and am a good networker. Forming relationships with a lot of individuals from many walks of life provided an opportunity to find a job. Of the career-focused jobs I have had, only one came about via a cold application, meaning I did not have any connections with anyone at the organization. Every other job relied on connections.

Connections are important for everyone, regardless of appearance. For a fat person, they are monumentally important. This reality can be very difficult for fat people who struggle with relationships or sociability. It is my opinion that a contributing factor to the number of extremely obese people who rely on social welfare programs is their inability to find employment, despite their best efforts. The combination of physical and emotional pain becomes too much to bear. Plus, they may not have the fortitude to press through discriminating barriers.

I won't bore you to death with a timeline of my professional career. Suffice it to say it's a messy timeline. I am grateful for the jobs I have had and for my current job – which is writing this book! My work, I believe, speaks for itself. The difficulty is finding someone to look past what they see so there's a chance for them to truly see my work ethic and job capabilities. As a fat person, I know the obstacles. I can choose to let them keep me down, or I can choose to rise above. It's not easy, but I choose the latter.

I do want to address one other area related to this topic – college. I began college right out of high school with high hopes. I ended up being on the eighteen-year graduation plan. By the time I finally had degree in hand, I was thirty-six years old. I had accumulated enough college credits (and debt) for at least one master's degree, maybe more.

I couldn't make up my mind about what I wanted to do with my life. I vacillated often, frequently changing programs and colleges. I take every opportunity I get to encourage young people to NOT do what I did. There were circumstances that contributed to my struggle as well. And as you've probably guessed, my weight was chief among them.

Many high school seniors look toward college with excitement. Even if they aren't academic nerds, many are excited about the college experience and everything it entails: parties, activities, new friends, sports, musical opportunities. All these experiences seem like a lot of fun. For many, the period of four to five years in college will be like no other time in their lives.

I was scared; terrified, really. The idea of living in a dorm was especially terrifying, because of my weight. In my college era (1990s), freshmen generally were required to live on campus. They were also required to live in the dorms built before the turn of the century. The nice dorms were reserved for upper classmen.

The dorm where I would be living consisted of four floors with a single bathroom for each floor. All the memories of gym class showers and the awful bullying and name-calling flooded my mind. I worried if the bed would hold me. I worried about whether I would fit in with a new crowd of people I didn't know.

Unfortunately, those worries ended up being validated during my first year. My fear of public restrooms intensified. I did anything and everything I could to be in and out of the shower before anyone else. I usually climbed out of bed at five a.m. or earlier to make sure I was alone. My bed held me just fine and my roommate was a good guy. He was the only one I connected with, though. I had dreams of becoming involved in campus musical groups and activities but didn't join because of fear of rejection. I found myself increasingly isolated.

What I am describing is a classic example of how my weight controlled aspects of my life for so many years. In this case, it prevented me from being able to relax and enjoy myself. I was filled with worry and anxiety. I popped anti-diarrheal medicine like candy!

After one semester, I felt like I couldn't take it anymore, so I returned to Michigan and made plans to transfer to a different college. That doesn't necessarily sound like a bad thing, except I gave up a full-ride scholarship. My college education would have been paid for so long as I maintained a 3.0 GPA. My inability to cope with my weight problem and its impact on my life led me to give that up and instead pursue seventeen years of on again/off again college education, a lot of debt, and a lot of heartache before I FINALLY graduated from college in 2012.

I'm not sharing this as a sob story. I'm sorry if it sounds that way. I did a lot of sobbing during the difficult years that followed my decision to let go of that scholarship! Being fat wasn't the actual cause of my decision; it was my inability to accept who I was and to love myself despite being fat that caused the fear and anxiety. There are other factors, but I believe my weights was the root problem that led to the bad decision to give up that scholarship and other bad decisions related to my education that followed.

My educational path caused issues with my career. I didn't really know what career I was going to have in the first place. I studied music for a few years because I love music and know I have a gift. Anxiety and poor self-esteem squashed that dream, and I found myself dropping out after three years of music studies because of burn-out and financial stress.

When I returned to college several years later, I decided to be a schoolteacher. I enjoyed teaching and thought it was a good fit. My anxiety and poor self-esteem squashed that endeavor, too. I couldn't handle the snickers and snide remarks from students about my weight. I chose to believe what I heard whispered by some teenagers and gave up that pursuit.

In between these educational pursuits, I did land two good jobs. I did some neat things: press conferences with governors, being on TV, authoring major publications, and helping advance important legislation. My insecurities boiled beneath the surface during all those successes. Somehow, I managed to pull it off without most people noticing, other than the occasional broken chair incident that clearly drew attention to my never-ending weight problem.

In the end, I credit my wife with helping me find the willpower necessary to finally finish my degree. It wasn't easy. I was working full-time, getting married, moving, and a lot of other things while attempting to finish my classes. I finally did it, though, and I was very proud.

It was also during this period that I began to gain weight again. Some well-meaning friends have tried to convince me it was the stress of life that led to the weight gain. I imagine stress was part of the problem. The challenges I have described in this chapter and the thoughts that contributed to those challenges are the root cause of my weight problem, though. It takes constant and continual psychological work and commitment to make healthy choices.

Today, I find myself in an interesting place in terms of my career. I'm still working in the field I've worked in for many years now – communications. It is work that I enjoy, and the causes I have worked for and that I do work for are important to me. I'm just beginning to also realize that I'm an author. Even though I have written for journals, newspapers, periodicals, and a whole host of other media, I never thought of myself as an author. Will this be a new career? I am confident there are more books in the pipeline. If you like this one, please keep that in mind (and tell all your friends, too!).

16

God Must Hate Me Because I'm Fat

"Jesus, loves me, this I know..."

Love is probably the most important tenet of the Christian faith. I've sat through hundreds of Sunday School classes and sermons about God's love. I've sung hundreds of songs out of a hymn book about God's love. I was taught using deformed looking stick figures on the flannel graph board that Jesus loved me so much, he died for me, and that God sacrificed his son because he loved me so much.

My head may have heard it. As an adult, I understood (at least in concept) the theology. My heart never believed it, though. God and I have a unique relationship; I've thought for years that God hates me. I am reminded of the scene in the movie *Bruce Almighty* where Jim Carrey's character says, "Smite me, oh thou great smiter!" I've had that conversation with God (maybe using slightly different vernacular) on many occasions.

Perhaps you don't consider yourself a spiritual being. That's okay. And please, keep reading. Don't worry. I'm not a theologian. I'm not going to try to convert you to Christianity or throw all sorts of Scripture your way. What I am going to share are my experiences growing up fat in a Christian environment, and how that experience damaged my view and understanding of God. Truth be told, many things from my experience growing up as the pastor's kid damaged my view of God. The most significant damage was caused by God's people – the church.

Before I go any further, though, I want to be sure to communicate something very important. This chapter is mostly about my struggles with the church, due to my unique place in life as an extremely fat son of a minister. The church is a wonderful and beautiful place, and there have been many wonderful and beautiful moments in my life because of being part of the church. I love the church; I just think it's important to try and communicate some of the challenges those of us outside the norm, when it comes to size, face in an effort to increase understanding and compassion.

I'm not certain when I first realized that my size apparently impacted my spirituality and my relationship with God. I know I was quite young when I began to realize that people in the church (skinny people, anyhow) seemed profoundly concerned about my weight. I imagine some of the concern was because of the potential damage to my physical body. Most, however, was related to my spiritual condition. Apparently, being fat meant I was somehow displeasing to God and headed toward hell if I didn't do something about it.

Suffering the double curse of being fat and being the pastor's son was like wearing a big sign that read, "PICK ON ME, PICK ON ME!" Church kids didn't need much encouragement. I learned early in life that church kids are some of the meanest on the planet. I endured as much teasing and verbal assault from kids in the church as I did from kids in school. Adults in my church, to my recollection, never intervened or came to my defense in any fashion. I suspect it's because they, too, believed what the kids were saying. They would often laugh and make some comment of their own about my weight.

My weight also caused moments of flat out embarrassment in the church. Some of the most significant embarrassment occurred during summer church camps. Camp is supposed to be fun, and I did have moments of fun. But I also had a lot of moments that weren't so fun because of my weight.

In the 1980s in the church I grew up in, most kids went to two camping programs that ran back to back. One was in Ohio and the other was in Michigan. My dad usually led music at the one in Ohio. This meant I got to stay with him, at least until I was a teenager, which was good because I had the comfort of being with someone I knew. The camp in Michigan was like the ones we see in movies. Kids descended from across the Midwest, and frazzled counselors attempted to keep us in line and impart Biblical teachings into our lives.

By this point in my life, I was fully aware that I was different from just about everyone else. I definitely took the bottom bunk. I was terrified of the camp restrooms and showers. I remember being chased around by bullies in the shower who backed me into a corner and threw stuff at me while snapping me with towels and calling me names. Sounds lovely and Christian, doesn't it? I was so paranoid about being seen naked by my peers that I would leap out of bed an hour before everyone else so I could shower and get dressed before anyone else was awake. This also contributed to my lifelong phobia of public restrooms.

Camp in Ohio was relatively uneventful. It is painful now to look at pictures and see what looks like Andre the Giant amidst a sea of normal kids. I was at least twice as wide as everyone else. Still, the experience in Ohio was mundane compared to the experience in Michigan.

Camp in Michigan was much more rustic. And I was on my own and responsible for my own defense most of the time. It's rarely a good thing for a pacifist child to be responsible for his own defense. The other kids at camp were supposed to be pacifists, too, since our church was a pacifist church. For some reason, many of them seemed to miss the memo on pacifism.

I recall one summer, probably when I was eight or nine years old, that was particularly embarrassing and painful. The camp had canoes, and in order to go out in one, a boat safety course was required. We were assigned to teams of three or four and led out into the swimming area of the lake. I was already on alert and embarrassed because I was in a swimsuit. Ladies, I understand your pain when it comes to swimsuits. Guys normally don't think anything about it, but I know many women fret over swimsuit selection. I didn't fret over my swimsuit; I fretted over the lack of a shirt when entering the water. My man boobs were on display, and I heard about it.

We climbed in the boat with a counselor, paddled around a bit, learned some of the basics, and then the counselor hopped out and flipped the boat over. We were all underneath the boat and were being taught what to do if our canoe tipped over. At first, it was kind of fun. It was an eerie yellow green color due to the content of toxic algae in the lake water. The counselor began to sing, "We all Live in a Yellow Submarine," which made perfect sense due to the hazy yellowness of everything around us. Then, the moment of truth arrived. I had seen other groups before us, so I knew what was coming next.

At the counselor's word, we all heaved the boat upward and attempted to flip it back over right side up. I was the only boy, and I was a weak boy. Our attempt was less than stellar. I was immediately smacked in the head (hard) by one of the bars in the boat. As it flipped, we didn't get it far enough out of the water, meaning that a good deal of water went into the boat in the process. Clearly, I was not man enough to flip the boat like the other guys who had no trouble. Of course, there were usually at least two guys in the groups that pulled it off successfully. That didn't matter at all when I brought that up during later sessions of teasing.

The flippage portion was not the worst, by far. What came next (after we bailed the water out of the boat) surpassed any other moments of embarrassment that camping year. We were now supposed to heave ourselves into the boat. I imagine most of you have probably seen something like this (think about those hilarious camping movies with the likes of Chevy Chase) and realize it's not a graceful process for many people. It's especially not a graceful process for someone who is two to three times larger than everyone else.

The two girls in my group easily leapt into the boat. They were like graceful gazelles. Now it was the rhinoceros' turn. I grabbed the bar in the center of the boat as instructed and heaved with all my might. The boat promptly tipped over dumping the gazelles back in the water. They were not amused. The boat also flipped over, and we were once again trapped in the yellow submarine. Back to square one.

We heaved a second time. I was a bit more determined at this point (trying to save whatever face I could) and we managed to get less water in the boat this go-around. The gazelles easily catapulted themselves back in the boat. It was now my turn again. I planted my hands and heaved for all I was worth, but this time was cognizant to try and balance the pressure on the bar so the boat wouldn't flip. I remained motionless with my feet planted squarely on the bottom of the lake. I heaved some more, strained some more, made grunting noises, and probably farted, which, thankfully, went unknown to anyone around me because my butt was in the water. I didn't move. I was like a cement block. My chubby body was not going to get in that boat no matter how hard I tried.

This entire episode was being viewed by my fellow campers, who were gathered along the dock or on the shore to watch. I began to hear the snickers of laughter. The counselor, after watching me attempt to get in the boat two or three times simply said, "Well, I guess you would drown. You probably shouldn't go out in a canoe." Good to know. To this day, I refuse to step foot in a canoe unless it's on a calm river that is less than three feet deep.

Experiences such as this one (and many more like it) gradually convinced me over the years of my childhood and youth that God must hate me. In my little kid brain, any type of spiritual experience equated with God. Thus, church was God, church camp was God, Christian school was God. I didn't separate spiritual events, experiences and activities from God. Since many of these experiences were painful and embarrassing, I began to believe that God must hate me because I was so different. I didn't know who or what to blame, so I blamed God.

My camp experiences were not the only difficult spiritual moments in my life. Church was never a safe place for me. Nearly every church event was accompanied by some type of painful experience related to my weight. Sometimes it was my inability to participate in activities at the same level as others. This usually resulted in derision from my peers. Sometimes it was being forced to eat an apple after kids' choir practice, while the rest of the kids got to eat cookies, cakes, or some other sweet treat. After all, "gluttony is one of the seven deadly sins, and we don't want you to go to hell, so this is in your best interest." I heard some version of that every week from the director as she dutifully handed me my apple.

Sometimes it was something even more overt, like the woman at church who snatched the piece of pie back out of my hand at the church potluck and told me "it's for your own good, I'm saving you from the pit." Of course, everyone nearby heard the exchange and saw me run off with tears rolling down my face, even though I was a teenager and wasn't supposed to cry anymore.

Sometimes it was the lecture I received from an adult at church, or the paranoia and fear I felt when I was worried someone in the church might come to my parents and give them a hard time about my weight telling them it wasn't a good reflection on the pastor or the church. I felt responsible for my dad's ministry to the church and blamed myself if someone left who I feared had made comments like these to my parents.

In the midst of these painful experiences, my weight did create some humorous moments. I spent a great deal of time at church, so it's only natural that crazy or unexpected things sometimes would occur. I broke chairs, I broke a piano bench or two, I ripped open my pants – all standard fare. Some of the more unique experiences involved my interaction with church people.

I recall one incident when a young girl, perhaps five years old, was visiting her grandmother. The little girl lived in West Virginia and had the sweetest southern drawl you had ever heard. After the service, she just kept staring at me. I'm sure I probably looked extremely huge in her eyes, and she seemed mesmerized.

I started a conversation with her grandmother, who took the opportunity to introduce us. I bent down to shake her hand and say hello, and she looked at me with the sweetest, most innocent eyes and said, "How come y'all's got two chee-ins (chins)?"

At first, I was caught off guard. Then I started laughing. Her grandmother was horrified. I came up with some lame response and reassured the grandmother that it was alright. Truth be told, deep down it hurt. I was an anomaly even to a five-year-old girl.

All the condemnation and confusion about my spirituality played out regularly at that sacred rite – the church potluck. For those who may not attend church or have an affinity towards casseroles, let me explain the church potluck. A potluck is the church's version of a Chinese or steakhouse buffet, replete with the separate area (usually a table) for desserts. The word "potluck" is especially appropriate because many of the food items arrive in pots of various sizes and colors, and you never quite know exactly what is inside until they are opened. The contents sometime remain a mystery even after they are opened.

There are standard potluck staples: scalloped potatoes, baked beans, macaroni and cheese, green bean casserole… these tasty, and calorie-laden carb bombs nearly always make an appearance. Some people specialize in jello salads. The word "salad" is especially deceptive, since these wondrous creations are generally filled with nuts, fruit, the ubiquitous celery, and loads of whipped cream. Lettuce is clearly lacking.

I know nothing about the history of potlucks. I do recall hearing pastors say more than once that potlucks were scriptural, because there are many examples in the Bible of people gathering around food. This is especially true with Jesus himself.

Apparently, Christ liked to eat. There are many references to him hanging out at various meals and parties. Jesus was probably one of the most well-liked guests at the potlucks of his day. Nothing to drink? No problem – bring me that water, and we'll really get this party going. Not enough food for the crowd? If Jesus was one of your guests, you didn't need to worry. Jesus also didn't have to fret and stew the night before trying to figure out what to bring.

Potlucks send mixed messages to fat people and turn the church into a hypocritical enabler. I can hear the cries of disagreement rising from among my Christian brethren. Please, hear me out. Potlucks in and of themselves aren't a bad thing. I'm all for Christian fellowship and gathering at a common table is a great way to do that. However, some churches take it to an extreme, with a potluck nearly every week. Let me enlighten you to what it's like for a fat person to approach a potluck.

The "luck" part of potluck probably means the most to most fat people. It's our lucky day! Hallelujah, we can eat all sorts of high-calorie, yummy, delicious food all at once! When I saw the potluck items being laid out at church, my stomach would rumble, and I would begin to salivate. I couldn't wait to get my hands on the lasagna (a rarity in our house) and the meatballs (never present in our house). And that was just the beginning.

When I was a kid, I would usually try to be one of the first through the line. By the time I was an adult, I would hang back, for two reasons. First, I remember plenty of adults chastising me for being at the front when I was young, often with comments such as "you better go to the back and give everyone else a chance." Second, I was trying to save face. It's one of those masks. I wanted everyone to believe I wasn't REALLY interested in all that food, while inside, I was shaking with excitement and drooling like crazy.

At my church, there was a distinct methodology. You grabbed a brown plastic tray, plopped the plate on top, and grabbed cutlery, napkin, etc. Then, you chose which side of the counter you wanted to walk on, but that really didn't matter because everything was within reach. I would heap so many things on my plate that it was often difficult to carry the tray and my drink in the other hand because my tray was so heavy.

When it came to dessert, I was always afraid the good stuff would be gone, so I didn't wait. I would set my overloaded plate down and head to the dessert table. Usually, I would take at least one of everything and fill another plate just with dessert items. I always noticed the disapproving stares. It wasn't unusual for someone to say something, even when I was an adult. One time I approached the dessert table for a second piece of pie that I really liked and jokingly said to an elderly woman that it was so good I was going to have a second piece. She looked right at me and said, "That would be a sin, wouldn't it?" She wasn't joking.

The potluck issue that trumps all other issues is that for fat people who have no sense of portion control, it truly becomes a grazing experience. I would wolf down the food on my plate and quickly return before something that I really liked was gone. Later in life, I was more discreet. I would grab and eat, especially the desserts.

What I mean by that is I would whisk by the table and quickly grab brownies, cookies, a piece of cake, a piece of pie, and I would shove it in my face while walking toward the kitchen. When I arrived in the kitchen, I would throw the plate away and head past the table another time. I'd grab something, sit down and eat it (always pretending it was the first item I had eaten) and then throw the plate away, whisk by the table again, and onward into the kitchen. Do you see the pattern?

I, like many fat people, do not have self-control when it comes to portions. We also do not have the traditional "full" signal that most people have. Our full signal is extreme pain in our stomachs. That's about the only time I would finally stop eating. That still didn't mean I was done, though.

Sitting for a few minutes allowed the volume of food in my gut to settle, and then I could restart the grazing process. I have no doubt that I easily consumed 6,000 to 8,000 calories at every potluck. When it was over, I would go home and sleep for three hours. Sometimes, it was difficult to make it in the door of the house, not because I was too wide, but because I was too tired from the sugar crash.

When I am actively losing weight or keeping it off, I have to practice evasive maneuvers on potluck Sundays. Typically, I would bring a healthy item (usually salad) and would load my plate up with that and allow only one spoonful (as in tablespoon, not serving spoon) of any of the fat-laden dishes. I avoided any interaction with the dessert table, especially if Ruby Lawler made her pecan pie. I would ride my bike to church or schedule a walk after the potluck to be sure to burn off any unintentional calories. For the most part, these habits have stuck with me, and I now approach potlucks with a much more open mind and a much more closed mouth. But on many occasions, I simply leave and don't participate. The temptation is too great.

Even though the church preaches love, and even though I heard about it repeatedly from the pulpit, in Sunday School, and plenty of other places, it wasn't long before it was firmly engrained in my psyche; God hates me. I didn't ask to be born fat. I didn't know why I ate so much. It must be because God hates me. I was going to go to hell for being fat. That was my punishment for being a sinner and because God hated me, that was my fate. I grew increasingly angry and bitter toward God and the church. Remember, in my mind, I didn't separate the two.

Fat people wear masks, and the Christians I hung out with at the time probably had no idea that inside, I truly believed God hated me and I was angry. I was very angry at what I saw as my curse in life. Interestingly, my experience, although a bit unique because of being a pastor's child, is nearly universal among fat Christians. Low self-esteem and self-worth along with a feeling of helplessness nearly always result in feeling as if God hates us.

So, how can the church respond? What can skinny people do? Is it best to just not say anything at all to your fat church mates?

Spritualty is complex. I can't sit here and say, "do this or don't do that" and guarantee it will make any difference. I do know that fat kids need to be loved and to be reminded continuously that they have value and worth and are loved by God. Believe me, they doubt it. It seemed like people in my dad's church were constantly coming at me with words of chastisement, diet plans and ideas that didn't make much sense to a kid. Too many times a well-meaning adult took me aside and said something like this.

"I'm only telling you this because I love you and I'm concerned. God is displeased with how you are living your life. I'm sure you know that gluttony is one of the seven deadly sins, and if you have sin in your life, that's going to keep you separated from God. I found this (insert name of latest diet fad) program, and I think it could really help you. Maybe this will help. And remember, if you stick to this and lose weight, God will be so happy, and you won't have to worry about continuing to displease him with your sinful gluttony."

These conversations probably began when I was eight or nine years old, and continued throughout the years, including when I was an adult. Looking back, what really stands out is that some people in the church felt it was their right to take me aside and say something. I've said for years that pastor's kids often endure being parented by the entire church.

It's a treacherous balance beam to walk because many church members feel entitled to say whatever they want to the pastor and his/her family, knowing that it's unlikely they'll get any pushback. In small churches like the ones my dad pastored, losing even a person or two because they get angry about something can make a huge difference. Thus, my siblings and I were programmed to listen passively and maintain peace, no matter what. This is further indication of how warped the world becomes when your family's livelihood depends on keeping certain people happy or making them feel validated about their "spiritual" insights and savvy.

It's taken longer and been a much more intentional process to figure out that God doesn't hate me. Some days, I'm still not so sure. I tend to see the scriptures related to smiting, and not see the scriptures related to loving. I tend to see myself as an outcast; someone abandoned by God for no clear reason. I remind myself daily that I am fearfully and wonderfully made (hold on...it's only a little bit of scripture/theology, and I promise to move by it quickly!), and I'm created in God's image.

Apparently, God must have a fat side. He must love fat people too, because we are everywhere, and I can't believe God hates us all. I do think God expects us to take care of ourselves and to cherish the life and body he has given us. He loves me no matter what, but my desire to be healthy is also fueled by my desire to be faithful to God.

PART 3

You'll Change

"We may encounter many defeats,
but we must not be defeated."
— Maya Angelou

17

Yo-Yo Hell

Most fat people experience yo-yo hell – that state of forever being on the yo-yo string when it comes to weight. Up and down, up and down, SWINGING AROUND LIKE CRAZY, hopping along the ground at your lowest weight for a few years with confidence like a "walking dog." (That's a reference that yo-yo geeks will get. The rest of you will have to Google it.) Yo-yo hell sucks. It sucks royally. Statistically, more than ninety-five percent of people who lose one hundred pounds or more will gain their weight back… and usually a few pounds more.

I'd like to say that I'm the exception. Believe me, I'd REALLY like to say that I'm the exception. For about three years, I was absolutely convinced that I would be in the five percent of people who didn't gain their weight back. I knew others who were in this group. They were my friends. Some were my very close friends. I spoke at dozens of events around the state and wrote blogs and articles for countless publications about how I would NEVER go back to how I was before.

I started a Facebook group called "We are the 5%" that was supposed to be an accountability tool for members who had lost one hundred pounds or more. Deep inside, I think I was being as public as I could be about my weight for accountability purposes. I was terrified about gaining my weight back. TERRIFIED. I would have dreams about being fat again. I would push aside nearly any obligation that got in the way of my exercise. I was NOT going to go back to being 430 pounds.

I distinctly recall the day when my yo-yo began its upward journey again. If I had put the kibosh on it right then and there, I might have been able to continue "walking my dog." But as is so often the case, I caved during a moment of weakness.

I was scheduled to speak and lead a walk at an event in Lansing. Unfortunately, as I headed into the city, I was hungry. It had been a very busy stretch with speaking events and fitness activities nearly every weekend. I would eventually move to Lansing, but at this time I was still driving seventy miles or more round trip to participate in these events, and they often started early in the morning. I was exhausted. Being exhausted and hungry is one of the most dangerous places for fat people to be.

On top of that, I basically had no food in the house. I grabbed an apple or something like that and headed out the door. I went to the event, spoke, walked, and left. By that time, it was past noon, and I was ravenously hungry. Being ravenously hungry is a VERY dangerous place for fat people to be.

As I headed out of town, I saw a local convenience store that is one of Lansing's most loved institutions. The company has operated a dairy for years and is known for their milk, ice cream, and bakery – especially their donuts.

You may recall from a previous chapter that donuts are my most significant vice and the recipient of my most profound love and attention. This particular chain of stores has, by far, the best donuts in Michigan, and perhaps in the entire nation. I knew this. I had known it for a long time. I had purposely refused to enter a one for three years.

That day, I was weak. I was hungry. I was tired. I was sick of eating fruits and vegetables. I wanted a donut, and I was going to get one. For the average person, this is not an issue. Even very healthy people eat donuts. In fact, it's become increasingly popular to sponsor "donut runs" as a fundraising event, where participants run a 5k or half-marathon eating a donut at each mile mark along the way. An occasional donut, especially for a truly healthy person, is not going to kill them. However, I was not a typical healthy person. My relationship with donuts was anything but platonic. I was treading on very dangerous ground.

I walked in and made a beeline for the donut case. The company had recently introduced a line of donuts known as "Primes." I didn't know about Primes until that very moment, but in the ensuing months, quickly came to know way too much about them. Primes are bigger, fatter, creamier, and have the wonderful distinction of being calorie bombs packing at least one thousand calories per donut, if not more.

As I stared at the donut case, all sorts of thoughts were running through my mind. I felt like I was in an episode of *Looney Tunes* with the devil on one shoulder and the angel on the other. I knew that donuts were my crack. I knew that crack addicts, alcoholics, and all other addicts must maintain complete sobriety. There can be no occasional indulgence, because one indulgence opens the floodgates all over again. I didn't care. I wanted a donut.

Donuts aren't illegal. One donut won't hurt me. You can control this, Jon. You've become much better about controlling your food urges. You can do this. It won't hurt. LIES!!! LIES STRAIGHT FROM THE PITS OF HELL!! This is what the angel was screaming at me.

221

I reached into the donut case and grabbed a Cappuccino Prime donut, which was basically a huge square donut filled with coffee flavored cream and coated with coffee flavored icing. I could feel its weight in my hand. It felt good. OK, only one Jon…only one. That's fine. Just not six, eight or twelve…only one. I approached the counter with my sin in its bag. I was trembling (not exaggerating). I was feeling waves of excitement running through my body. I was also in the process of abruptly ending my dog walk and beginning the upward yank on my yo-yo.

I returned to my car and bit into the creamy deliciousness of that donut. When I finished, a thought immediately entered my mind. "There are more of these stores in Lansing. Before you leave town, you could stop and get another." And that's what I did. The downward spiral that would lead to the upward swing in my weight had begun.

That donut led to more, and more, and more. I fought valiantly, and for a while, I was able to keep the beast at bay because I continued to exercise continuously. My weight crept upward very slowly. I would admonish myself, swear off the donuts, and the weight would creep back downward. A vicious cycle was underway – the vicious cycle of yo-yo hell.

It took several years, but I eventually gained back more than one hundred pounds. Along with that gain came the medicines needed to treat high blood pressure and diabetes. I felt like a failure. I was depressed. Thankfully, I eventually realized that I was still in the driver's seat, and I didn't have to accept a death sentence due to obesity. I'm more realistic about the struggle these days. I know what I must do, but in the midst of doing it, I'm also learning to be kind to myself when I mess up. That's a key component of staying out of yo-yo hell.

For some, yo-yo hell is an extended process. It may mean several years at a healthy weight, followed by several at an unhealthy weight, followed by several at a healthy weight, and perhaps there are only three or four rides on the yo-yo throughout a lifetime. For others, the swings are much more frequent, but not as dynamic. Up ten pounds, down twenty pounds, up twenty pounds, down ten pounds...you get the idea.

Both types of yo-yo hell are emotionally exhausting and physically destructive. Those who experience the large swings are the most prone to physical issues as a result. Research has shown that over time frequent yo-yo dieting and the swings that are involved can wreak havoc on the body's metabolism and weight-control mechanisms.

I would like to give you my best advice on this subject. Are you ready? Here it comes:

DON'T DO IT!

I could end this chapter right here, except I know that those three words are much easier said than done. Recall the statistic I mentioned earlier – nearly ninety-five percent of individuals who lose one hundred pounds or more will gain it back, and often gain even more. The odds aren't in our favor.

Why? Why is it that some people can successfully avoid yo-yo hell? If I had the answer to that, I'd be a millionaire. I believe it's because extreme obesity is largely a psychological problem. Like many psychological problems, there is no permanent cure. It is necessary each and every day to follow routines and pay attention to thoughts, feelings, and emotions while understanding how to cope with them in healthy ways in order to stay on track. This is a difficult process and can often be emotionally overwhelming in and of itself.

I also believe knowledge is power. In this case, that means I think it's important to understand and realize the challenge of maintaining a large weight loss. Just like many extremely obese people think they will be the exception to the inevitable negative health consequences of being fat, many begin a weight loss journey convinced they will be able to keep it off forever. The odds are against them. The odds are against me, too. And unfortunately, I became one of the majority and not the minority.

I don't say this to be negative. A positive outlook and believing in your ability to overcome your weight challenges is very important. But I don't think it's helpful to be Pollyannaish either. I know people who have successfully maintained their weight loss. I probably know a lot more than the average person because of the circles I worked within after losing 230 pounds. I also know the pain of the yo-yo. The bottom line is it's important to be aware of the odds that you are up against. Never give up. Keep trying. Pull that yo-yo string back down and into the walking dog position with all your strength and might. I, and thousands of others, are on the journey with you.

18

Denial and Truth

It's impossible to live life as a 400-plus pound human without denial. I should know. I spent many years in the 400-plus range and spent a bunch more in the 300s. Some of you will disagree. You will say, "That's not true – I'm happy with myself, and I deny nothing." I will say you are lying. I don't say that to be mean. You may not even realize you are lying, because of your denial. Denial is complex and its roots, once entangled in our brain, psyche, spirit – wherever it happens to be residing – are very difficult to uproot and remove.

There are many types of denial. Depending on what you read, where you look, and how studious you happen to be, the number of types may vary, as will the label or description. I began in the place that all research should begin – Google. From there, I immediately jumped to the bastion of all worldly knowledge – Wikipedia.

Wikipedia lists six types of denial that I have summarized and renamed based on my experience:

Deny the facts – avoid the facts by lying to yourself and others.

Deny responsibility – avoid personal responsibility by blaming, minimizing, or justifying behavior, or attempt to shift responsibility to someone else. This is the classic, "It's not my fault!"

Deny impact – refuse to acknowledge the consequences of actions on yourself or others.

Deny awareness – blame behavior on drugs, alcohol, busyness, trauma or something else that altered your state of mind and basic ability to pay attention to your own life.

Deny the cycle – avoid looking at what causes the problem or leads up to an event. "It just happened."

Deny denial – remain confident that nothing needs to change because you see and understand the problem (what problem?) clearly.

Fat people operate with every one of these types of denial in place. Breaking through denial is probably the most difficult change that has to be made to find both physical and mental health. Please, trust me on this one. I'm an expert at denial. A day rarely goes by that I don't catch myself in some form of it, and I have to really think through my behaviors and actions to eradicate it.

Each of the above types were evident in my own behaviors. Oops, I just realized I wrote a sentence with closeted denial. Notice my choice of the word "were" instead of "are." Yep, uprooting denial is a daily chore. Denial will likely never go away completely, especially if you've been immersed in it for most of your life. Don't despair. You can overcome a lot of its effects.

What does denial look and sound like? Let me give you specific examples:

Deny the facts – "I'm not fat; I'm pleasingly plump."

Deny responsibility – "It's not my fault I'm fat. It's in my genes, and my parents only made it worse by teaching me unhealthy eating habits."

Deny impact – "My health isn't affected by my weight at all. I may be big, but I'm healthy!"

Deny awareness – "I only overeat at restaurants. The rest of the time, I eat like everybody else."

Deny the cycle – "I'm destined to be fat. I've been fat since day one. There's nothing I have done to deserve it. It's just my lot in life."

Deny denial – "I work sixty hours a week, am active socially, and have no trouble keeping up with my friends. I may be fat, but it doesn't affect my ability to do what I want."

Earlier, I said it's impossible to live life as a 400-plus pound human without denial. Why do I say that? Denial becomes a coping mechanism. Denial offers the fat person a way to live and interact with the world despite all the pain and turmoil.

Let's face it; everyone on this planet deals with some kind of denial. I'm not trying to single out only fat people, though the layers of denial that fat people build up outnumber the best lasagnas or baklavas! It took me a lot of years to realize that my denial was a mental illness linked to many other mental problems that were linked to my extreme obesity.

It's hard to recognize denial from within. Those who are on the outside are usually the ones to spot it. Think about it. Have you ever said to a close friend, "I think you're in denial." Probably. Most of us can spot it easily in others but overlook it completely in ourselves.

I don't think denial as a coping mechanism was fully formed in me until my early adult years. During my school years, I may have tried to deny that I was fat, but someone reminded me of the fact on pretty much a daily basis. As a kid, though, I didn't even think about the health consequences, relationship consequences, and all that other stuff that was going to be

227

majorly screwed up because of my weight. In 1980s America, only fifteen percent of the population was obese, and childhood obesity was a rarity. People picked on me and gave me a hard time because of how I looked but didn't say much about future consequences.

Looking back on my life now, it's easy to see some of the layers of denial I had in place internally, but also would occasionally exhibit externally. And I recall that more than one person called me out on some of them, but of course, I denied what they were trying to point out. Here are some examples.

First, I compared myself to those around me. I looked around and saw six foot five guys in their twenties who were thin as a rail and wolfing down at least as much, if not more food than me. Why shouldn't I be able to eat that way too? They can eat whatever they want; I should be able to eat whatever I want, too!

Look at me deny the facts and deny the impact. The fact is, I am five foot nine and come from a long line of stocky and obese people. Like it or not, my genes don't allow me to eat whatever I want and get away with it. It may make me angry, but that's the truth.

My refusal to accept the truth of the situation also led me to deny its impact. If I ate whatever I wanted, I was going to be extremely overweight. Being extremely overweight sucked and was going to create health complications, relationship issues, and make life pretty miserable overall.

Oh, but wait… that's not going to happen to me. I have some medicine that will keep my blood pressure under control. I'm still able to do the activities with my friends that I want to, so long as we don't go to amusement parks, movie theatres, climb mountains, snow ski, water ski, hang glide, or launch into space.

I'm fine. My weight doesn't impact my life at all, other than hurtful remarks from skinny people.

Wrong.

I sat on a bench and watched my friends climb some of those mountains. I still haven't seen the Upper Falls of Tahquamenon Falls in my home state of Michigan because I couldn't climb the stairs. I sat there while my friends took it all in.

I told myself blood pressure medicine, which I began taking when I was fifteen, would keep everything in check, and it's no big deal that I have to spend two hours in the bathroom after taking it. Oh, and why is it that the doctor has to keep increasing the dose? Man, they should come up with some better medicine than this stuff. This is the twenty first century! Where's the single pill that will save my heart, keep my joints from collapsing, make it easier to breathe, and remove all the self-hatred inside my head that is driving my behavior anyhow?

Yep. Deny impact, and really, denial of denial of denial of denial… deep, thick layers of lies and half-truths that I told myself in order to be able to wake up in the morning, face another day, and cope with being a 400-plus pound man in a 200-pound man world.

Have you ever noticed that nearly all fat people drink diet soda? Let me rephrase that; nearly all EXTREMELY fat people drink diet soda. People who are just slightly overweight may have a regular pop habit. Breaking that habit would likely result in them reaching a normal weight.

Many extremely fat people have an addiction to diet soda. It may be partially physical, as caffeine is an addictive substance. But it's mostly psychological. I can and do feel better about making bad food choices by telling myself I'm saving calories by choosing a diet soda. This is one of the most compelling examples of denying facts from my life and the life of many others who struggle with their weight.

I'm a creature of habit. Most of us are. Unfortunately, most of us are creatures of bad habits. We struggle to establish good habits, but have little trouble falling into bad ones. Once there, it seems ten times harder to break a bad habit than it did to develop it in the first place.

For years, I had a habit of stopping at McDonald's on my way home from work. I had a forty-minute commute, so I would go through the drive-thru every day. Often, my order was exactly the same. "I'd like four double-cheeseburgers and a large diet soda." The cheeseburgers were cheap. They pedaled their wares for rock bottom prices. Ninety-nine cent double cheeseburgers were the prostitute of fast food. I willingly partook.

What I didn't realize (and didn't care about at the time) was that those four double cheeseburgers were 440 calories each, with 23 grams of fat, 11 grams of saturated fat, and 1,050 mg of sodium. For those who are mathematically challenged, that totals 1,760 calories, 92 grams of fat, 44 grams of saturated fat, and 4,200 mg of sodium.

You may recall from school that adults are supposed to consume 2,000 to 2,500 calories per day, depending on gender, activity level, etc. Most experts recommend that men consume 2,500 calories, unless they exercise heavily, or their work requires lots of manual labor. I worked in a position that required only sitting on my butt. I was definitely in the 2,500-calorie category, at best.

Those four double cheeseburgers were 70 percent of my daily calorie needs. They were also 140 percent of my daily fat, 216 percent of my daily saturated fat, and 176 percent of my daily sodium needs. But wait a minute! I made a healthy choice, too!

Protein – that's important, AND... I got a diet soda. Choosing diet soda means that the whole fat-laden, artery-clogging, heart disease-causing, food choice DIDN'T matter! Denial. Deny the facts, deny responsibility, impact, cycle, and... then deny the denial.

Keep in mind folks that the trip through the drive-thru was only one eating episode in the course of the day. By the time I hit that drive-thru, I had mostly likely had donuts or Pop-Tarts for breakfast (if I ate breakfast), Chinese buffet for lunch, cookies or candy for snacks, and... when I made it home forty minutes later, it was time for dinner, which might easily be a 2,000 calorie mounded plate of spaghetti and meatballs.

Oh, and that's right, I'm supposed to meet my friend Bob at the coffee shop at eight o'clock. I'll have some donuts and a diet soda. In hindsight, it's easy to see that it wasn't unusual for me to consume 10,000 calories or more in a single day. Is it any wonder I had a weight problem?

The thought that what I was eating and how I was eating it might be contributing to my weight problem almost never crossed my mind because I denied the impact. It didn't matter. I was healthy. I was doing what I wanted to do and eating what I wanted to eat – just like everyone else. Being fat has no impact on me, other than putting up with those stupid people who say stupid things. They're jerks anyhow. Who cares?

Oh, and before I forget... back to breakfast. Take a poll of your fat friends, and I can pretty much guarantee you'll find a whole lot of breakfast skippers. After all, that's fewer calories, and that means it's a healthy choice, right?

Skipping breakfast means I have self-control. People always say that fat people have no self-control. Well, they're wrong. If I can skip breakfast, surely that's proof of my amazing self-control.

The truth is that readily available, peer-reviewed research has shown that not eating breakfast is extremely counterproductive. The truth is that fat people do struggle with self-control. Denying the truth isn't going to change the reality of what will occur.

I would like to say that I've mastered all of this and have overcome denial completely, but I would be denying my denial. Of course, I'm still in denial. In many areas facing the truth is hard, and I don't like doing it any more than anyone else. Even though I still struggle with denial, I will say that I now at least attempt to approach my thoughts, feelings, and decisions with the realization that my actions may reflect denial. Thankfully, my wife often catches the denial for me.

More recently, after a long struggle with trying unsuccessfully to keep my weight off after three years of success, I had to acknowledge that if I did not take specific steps to keep my weight down, I would likely shorten my life, and definitely shorten my ability to enjoy my life. Sometimes, life draws our attention to things that draw our attention to our denial.

For example, after losing 230 pounds in my early 30s, I developed fat-dar. No matter where I went, I would suddenly see all the fat people around me, especially the extremely fat people. Fat-dar had a way of landing on individuals who had probably nearly reached the end.

Fat-dar had a way of landing on the person in a motorized cart with legs bandaged because cellulitis from circulation problems and diabetes along with edema had gotten so bad that their leg exploded and was oozing built-up fluid that their tired and overworked hearts couldn't circulate out of their extremities. Fat-dar had a way of landing on the guy in the cart at the Chinese buffet who was shoveling in food so fast that those present could hear his heavy breathing and see the sweat on his forehead. Fat-dar had a way of landing on the woman with a cane hunched forward, struggling to even take one step. Fat-dar had a way of landing on the future Jon Stanton. It was a future that I was and am DETERMINED to avoid.

I had to break through the denial that it would somehow be different for me. I had to stop believing that I was the exception. Look around you, or think about your friends, family, and colleagues. Do you know any 400-pound seventy year olds? How about eighty? Have you ever seen a 400-pound person who was in their eighties and able to drive, walk, move, and have any type of meaningful life? Probably not. Most extremely fat people – people like me – rarely make it past their sixties. Denial told me that I would be that one-tenth of one percent. I had to wake up to reality.

The Truth

Why does the truth often seem so elusive? Why do we (or at least I) tend to stare truth right in the face and either deny its existence or refuse to acknowledge its presence?

I've heard and read a lot about truth. Much of this was a result of my Christian upbringing. Jesus had a lot to say about truth. In fact, he used the word a lot. I heard one verse often, but had a hard time grasping what it meant. "You shall know the truth, and the truth shall set you free." (John 8:32). Truth be told, the verse is pretty straightforward. It was my choice to make it more complicated than it really is. It took a lot of years before I finally allowed truth to begin to set me free.

Later in life, I read a book called *Telling Yourself the Truth* by William Backus and Marie Chapian. The book was part of my treatment plan from my therapist because I had a nasty habit of lying to myself. Those lies ran the gamut from denial, to disbelief, to downright deception, depending on the issue at hand. I am convinced that fat people continually lie to themselves in order to make it through a day and stay alive.

We lie to ourselves to avoid the painful truth that we hate ourselves. We hate our bodies. We hate our personalities. We hate our clothes. Fat people often hate their jobs. Fat people often hate their lives.

Are there exceptions? Of course. I have no data that says this is universally true for every single fat person. However, I have my own experience, and the experiences of hundreds of fat people I have talked to in recent years, and self-hatred is universally present. Self-hatred is wrapped up in thousands of lies that we have chosen to believe over the years. These are lies that we tell ourselves and lies that we hear from others around us that we choose to believe.

I know of only one way to attempt to find freedom from this bondage, and yes, it is bondage. You must look truth squarely in the face and work really, really hard to accept it, acknowledge it, and begin the very difficult process of counteracting the lies with the truth.

I'm a nerd and a geek and enjoy shows like *Star Trek* and movies such as the *X-Men,* mostly because of the cool special effects and awesome powers some of the characters possess. Believe me, there are days when I feel like a mutant, except I didn't receive any cool superpowers. The mutant I relate to most closely is The Blob, a mutant with so much body mass that he has his own gravitational field and can squish people at will. That might come in handy in certain situations, I suppose.

The reason I went down that incredibly weird path is because I sometimes visualize my battle to see, listen, and accept the truth, as being like a battle between good and evil. I have to pull out my "phaser," which shoots out little "truth beams" and zap the lies that come at me repeatedly. My phaser gets a lot of use. After more than thirty years of constructing lies and choosing to believe them, or hearing lies and choosing to believe them, that phaser is working double duty all the time.

The first truth that I had to accept was that being fat was going to kill me. The number one lie that fat people choose to believe is that they are somehow statistically different and being one hundred pounds or more overweight will not lead to an early grave. It will. Statistics and reality are NOT in your favor on this one. Again, there will obviously be a few outliers, but if you are one hundred pounds or more overweight, you will die earlier, and your last years are likely to be pretty miserable.

I first accepted this truth at the age of thirty-one. My doctor, a straight-shooter for the most part, diagnosed me with Type 2 diabetes and said, "If you don't do something about your weight, you're going to dead by the time you're fifty and the last ten years of your life will be complete misery." What? Dead by the time I was fifty? Wait a minute! My weight isn't a problem. I'm still healthy and able to do things I want. He's wrong. I'll be okay.

Except, he was right.

I had just been diagnosed with Type 2 diabetes. I already had high blood pressure and high cholesterol. I couldn't walk a city block, and my back hurt constantly. My weight WAS killing me. It was a slow and painful death. At that moment, I chose to face the truth and realize I was going to be miserable and die an early death if I didn't do something about it. This episode was my wake-up call.

I have yet to meet another person who has lost more than one hundred pounds who did not have a similar experience. It seems that a wake-up call is a necessary component of successful weight loss for an extremely obese individual. Without a wake-up call, a person may lose weight, but isn't likely to be consistent enough and dedicated enough for it to last in the long term.

My friend and mentor, Jodi Davis, often shares about her wake-up call. Jodi had been obese her entire life. She had reached more than three hundred pounds. Then, it was time to attend a funeral for one of her cousins. This particular cousin had also been obese her entire life. She died before the age of fifty from complications related to her weight. Jodi knew that going into the funeral but still couldn't face the truth of her own obesity. She would be the one that made it. Her cousin's death was a fluke. Being fat wasn't going to kill her.

During the funeral, Jodi watched as her cousin's teenage son stood over his mother's casket and wept. Suddenly, she realized her son might not have his mom with him when he graduated from high school, when he went to college, when he got married, when he started a family of his own. Jodi had kids – children she adored with all her heart. She immediately realized that she wasn't any different from her cousin. It was as if she was staring at her own casket at that very moment, and her children were weeping over the loss of their mother – her.

That was Jodi's moment. She went home and immediately began changing her lifestyle and her habits. Her kids became her motivation. Jodi chose to walk regularly and eat healthy meals and snacks. That was it. No magic pill, potion, diet, or surgery. She walked off 162 pounds. She's kept the weight off for more than fifteen years. Today, Jodi travels across the nation inspiring others to face the truth and change their lives for the better. Her efforts reached me, and I thank Jodi every opportunity I get for saving my life.

Jodi and I both had to accept the truth of our situations. Our wake-up calls were different, but the truth we were both denying was the same. At age thirty-one, I had to accept that my years were limited. I had to accept that my body was already damaged. I had to accept my own personal responsibility for my condition. Fat people generally carry with them a whole cadre of excuses as to why they are fat. My excuse book included things like: "It's in my genes; my whole family is fat" or "This is just who I am. I enjoy food. I enjoy eating. Why should I fight my natural inclinations?"

I had an eye-opening moment about excuses somewhere along the way while losing 230 pounds. Excuses aren't necessarily lies. They can be, but many excuses are in fact truth. There is a genetic component to being extremely overweight. There's also a genetic component to being a six foot five Adonis with a rippled six pack, huge muscles, and the ability to run three Ironmans in one weekend! I received the first set of genes. The second set of genes was somehow snuffed out by evolution in my family tree long ago, if they ever existed in the first place.

The excuse "It's in my genes" is in fact a true statement. The lie I told myself for years was that my genetic make-up meant it was completely valid for me to weigh 430 pounds. It was useless to fight my genes. This is generally the pattern that exists with excuses that are based in truth.

The underlying excuse is indeed true. We then use the truth to validate lies. Fighting genes, for lack of a better term, is difficult, no doubt. I gain weight just looking at a picture of donuts. In fact, it is my personal belief that I gain weight more quickly than just about anyone else I know. Losing weight, on the other hand is extremely difficult. I have to work much harder, toe the line with what I eat with no exceptions, or the weight comes back. These are genetic truths in my life, but I can't allow them to be excuses for being extremely overweight.

I also had a convenient way of denying the truth regarding that six foot five Adonis. Jealousy doesn't even begin to describe the emotion I felt in the presence of such an individual. Jealously usually gave way to rage at God, anger, depression, and a sense of total and complete failure in life. I would sit across the room and watch Adonis eat three times as much as I was eating and joke about how "he could eat so much, but just never seems to gain weight."

After such an encounter, I would generally head to the nearest donut shop for a dozen cream-filled long johns to cheer me up. I imagine some of you may be shaking your heads in agreement, while others of you may be shaking your head wondering why I would let something as simple as a good-looking, athletically fit person rock my world in such a profound way.

This example (which is only one of thousands my brain conjured up over the years) is a good one because it indicates the depth of deceit and lies that reside in the brain of a fat person. The person I observed who appeared to have it completely made in all aspects of his life may in fact have been an alcoholic, just diagnosed with cancer, a rageaholic, bi-polar, unemployed, mean and nasty, a jerk, or insert any other type of negative vice or human struggle. In other words, his physical appearance didn't necessarily mean his life was perfect, by any means.

My physical appearance made it abundantly clear that my life lacked balance and self-control. His physical appearance projected the opposite. Truth be told, he may indeed have been an extremely disciplined, balanced individual with loads of self-control. Here's the clincher: None of that matters.

The comparison game must end before anyone can successfully lose weight and keep it off. That's part of the psychological healing. No matter what I do, I cannot be six foot five. Duh. Why beat myself up continually about only being five foot nine? Any six pack I'm packing is so well insulated it won't ever be exposed to the elements. Could I someday have those wonderful six pack abs? Maybe. It would involve a knife, time in the hospital, and so much work and effort that I would probably have to neglect my wife, neglect my job, neglect all of my obligations and do nothing but exercise and eat grass and twigs for a couple of years. Yeah, that sounds like fun.

Here's the point that I am trying to make. I have to accept myself and love myself. You have to accept yourself and love yourself, too. No diet plan, motivational TV show, or exercise regimen is going to be successful in the long term if you do not stop comparing yourself to others and learn to love yourself. That's the truth, and that's the truth that will indeed set you free. If you are skinny and have never had a weight problem, but have a friend or loved one who does, remind them DAILY that they are loved and accepted.

I haven't fully arrived at this truth, by the way. Years of painful experiences and damage to my psyche must be worked through if I'm ever going to fully grasp this truth and own it. The funny thing is, I know that. As I sit here typing this, I know the truth of what I just wrote, yet I still find ways to deny it and allow negative thoughts about myself to control my actions. Owning the truth is not easy. It's very hard. It's probably the hardest thing I deal with in my life on a regular basis.

The pendulum can swing so easily. I spent nearly five years loving my life and the freedom that actively losing weight and then keeping it off and being healthy brought to my daily existence. I did things during that period that I never dreamed possible. I completed two half-marathons. I rode my bike one hundred miles in a single day and put more than three thousand miles on my bike every year for three years. I found the courage to pursue love. I found the strength and energy it takes to pay it forward and do my best to tell others about my experience and encourage them that they could do it too. I drove thousands of miles and spent all sorts of time and money trying to convince others about the freedom that comes from healthy living.

And then the pendulum swung. A little bit at first, but then faster and stronger as I gave in to old thoughts, old habits, old excuses, old lies. I gained weight. I lost my ability to do those things I had so recently done and felt so proud and strong for being able to do. Depression reared its ugly head. I floundered. I scrambled. I failed. Desperation set in. What had happened? Where was my willpower? Where was my desire to live? Why couldn't I stay on track for more than a week at a time?

You lazy, rotten, no good piece of garbage. You're never going to be successful. You might as well give up right now. Eat and enjoy it while you can because you'll be dead before you know it, and the world will be a better place.

Ouch. My truth phaser needs a new battery. I had a choice to make. I could continue the slow descent and find myself firmly entrenched in yo-yo hell, or I could begin zapping those lies once again. I could challenge my demons one at a time. I could tell myself the truth.

The truth is I will always struggle.

I will always have to work harder than many people around me.

I will always have to carefully watch what I eat and consistently exercise.

I will never be able to eat whatever I want and not suffer any consequences.

This is heavy stuff, and I have taken great pains to try and keep this book positive and humorous. Negativity breeds negative results. I feel compelled to be openly honest here, though, and to ask you to take a very hard look at yourself.

Maybe you don't have a weight problem, but your spouse does. Do you see your denial? Do you see their denial? It can be hard to spot. I encourage you to ask a trusted friend to make you aware. Recognizing and dealing with denial is imperative to establishing a healthy life.

I can allow the truth of my situation to be a millstone around my neck, or I can choose to accept the truth and live accordingly. Bondage or freedom – it's my choice, and it's your choice. The truth hurts, but freedom, as with most good things in life, comes with some pain and sacrifice.

Oh, and one last thing. NEVER give up. NEVER. There is always hope. Cling to it. Grasp on to that hope with all your strength, and NEVER, NEVER, NEVER give up!

19

Inspiration

If you're going to lose a lot of weight, you can't do it alone.

Fellowship is important.

Human beings are meant to be social.

Isolation is the number one enemy of the addict.

I have found each of these statements to be profoundly true. Fortunately, I'm a bit social by nature, most of the time. Ironically, isolation (which stands in stark contrast to being social) is something I have battled and continue to battle. If you are an addict or are close friends with an addict of any type, it's likely you have experienced or witnessed the tendency to isolate to avoid pain. For fat people, isolation is even more alluring because of the pain that often comes with being seen in social situations.

Being fat is often an exercise in extremes and for most of my adult life, I swung back and forth between sociability and isolation. I was usually viewed as the life of the party and had many friends and was involved in many activities. This busyness helped me avoid the pain of my situation, although there were times when things would occur in social settings that could send me into an isolationist tailspin. My friends and loved ones had a hard time understanding how someone who seemed to enjoy people so much could disappear or hole himself up in his house for periods of time, only to emerge later as if nothing had happened.

When I finally decided to address my weight problem, I figured out pretty early that I was going to have to find people to surround me and encourage me. I was living with my parents for a brief stretch due to being in school again when I first began my journey toward health. My sister Becka and her family were also living with my parents, as was my brother David. Yes, it was a very full house. Thankfully, I managed to exit rather quickly and get back out on my own. While living with my parents, my sister, who'd had bariatric surgery, helped me figure out what to eat, and what NOT to eat. I'm grateful for her help in getting me on the right track when it came to healthy food choices.

My mom has always been a walker, and she enjoyed taking walks with me in the evening once I was able to move beyond the end of the driveway. My mom is tall and has long legs. We're about the same height, but her height is in her legs, and my height is in my upper body. My short, stubby legs had to work overtime to keep up with her stride. I took at least two steps for every one step she took. At first, this was a source of consternation, but I eventually came to appreciate the extra work on my part since it burned more calories.

My friend Char also walked with me, in all sorts of places. I can't even begin to list all the places we walked because it would probably fill several pages. Char had even shorter legs than I, and due to her personality, she was frequently exasperated at my speed and distance. She mostly got over it though, and we had a lot of fun. We walked all over downtown Owosso where she lived regardless of weather conditions. We frequented the River Trails in Owosso and Lansing. If the weather was too miserable, we did laps inside of Meijer. I quickly made friends with many of the staff at the Meijer in Corunna, Michigan, and they became a bit of a cheering section as they witnessed the weight melt off my body.

Human beings are meant to be social. Outliers exist, but for the vast majority, this statement is true. Going it alone when it comes to trying to lose one hundred pounds or more is likely a recipe for disaster. Find friends, find loved ones, find strangers on the street, join a walking club, join a gym, join a class, join ANYTHING to get you involved with people who will help hold you accountable and offer support.

Perhaps you are the person who can be that support. Maybe you don't have a weight problem, but your friend or loved one does. Here's my advice to you:

Make it a priority to be available whenever and however possible – no excuses.

Fat people are used to hearing excuses from their skinny friends/loved ones about why they "can't do this or that with them," and we take it personally. Remember, we likely aren't psychologically healthy. Thus, your reason for not wanting to do something with us is because we are fat, and you don't want to be seen with us. Even if that statement is true, please, don't admit it. Get over yourself, and help your friend or loved one in need.

Several months into my weight loss experience, I happened to receive a copy of the magazine Living Healthy in the mail from my health insurance provider. On the cover was a picture of a person who would come to be one of my closest mentors and a

245

true friend to my wife and me. The first thing I noticed on that cover other than the smiling face were the words:

"Jodi Davis walked off 162 pounds and has kept it off. Find out her secret inside."

I did a double take. At that time, I had been walking and eating correctly for a few months and had already lost about sixty pounds. I opened the magazine and read a story remarkably like my own. Although we're different in that she's a few years older than me and has three wonderful children, Jodi (whom I also mentioned in the previous chapter) and I had very similar childhoods. Our experience with our weight was nearly identical, too. I knew I had to find a way to contact her. Thankfully, the article concluded with her website address. I quickly logged in, found her email address and sent her a message.

Jodi responded quickly and graciously. As the Healthy Living Advocate for Blue Cross Blue Shield of Michigan, Jodi not only had the website and the magazine article, she also had the opportunity to travel across Michigan promoting walking and sensible eating as a way to lose weight and keep it off. We began a dialogue, and I found a person who really understood what my life had been like and what it was like now.

Jodi offered lots of wonderful advice and encouragement. I am eternally grateful for her assistance. Later, when Jodi and I hit the road together to share our story with others in Michigan, I was quick to mention that I truly believed Jodi had helped to save my life.

After our initial electronic contact, I found out Jodi would soon be coming to Lansing. I took the opportunity to meet her, walk with her, and Jodi wrote an article about me for her website. Another great friend saw the value of our combined message, along with our knack for yak, and soon many events became "Jodi and Jon." The rest, as the saying goes, is history.

I loved every minute of it. We spoke at special health events, kicked off 5k races, walked with dignitaries, interviewed with media, made videos, and most importantly, inspired thousands to change their lives through walking and practical, every day means. Eventually, we both received the Charles T. Kuntzelman Award from Michigan Governor Jennifer Granholm. This award is given each year to three or four individuals in Michigan who have overcome obstacles with their health to encourage and inspire others to be healthy as well.

At some point during our first year on the road, Jodi mentioned that she had been on NBC's morning talk show, *Today*, in early 2008. She was the very first member of Joy Bauer's "Joy Fit Club." Jodi put me in contact with Joy, who quickly contacted me about an amazing opportunity.

Joy Bauer is a registered dietitian and the nutrition expert for *Today*, as well as many other organizations. Joy is also a best-selling author of several books related to diet and nutrition. At the time we met, Joy was working on her latest book, "The LIFE Diet®." (The LIFE Diet is also sold in paperback form as "Your Inner Skinny®.") She asked me if I was willing to follow the diet for a period of time leading up to my appearance on *Today*.

I hesitated at first because I am not a fan of diet plans. At that point in time, I had lost 180 pounds without any specific type of diet program. I just paid attention to what I ate, made healthy choices, and ate in moderation. I also exercised like crazy.

However, after talking to Joy about the plan, I agreed to check it out. What I soon realized is that the whole concept behind The LIFE Diet® was to establish healthy habits using real foods in real combinations without focusing exclusively on some particular type of food. In other words, I was basically already living the LIFE Diet®, without even knowing that it existed.

The LIFE Diet® did help me become more regimented in my patterns of eating, and it gave me access to many new and tasty recipes. I had already figured out every possible way to cook a chicken breast, and not being a natural in the kitchen, the recipes were very helpful.

I soon lost another fifty pounds. Having reached my lowest weight as an adult (201 pounds), I was booked to appear with Joy on *Today* in early January 2009. Ironically, I happened to be on a Caribbean cruise the week before the show, and everyone (including me) was worried I would gain weight during the cruise. After all, cruises are notorious for delicious foods and constant, continual eating. Knowing that I was about to appear before several million people on national television was powerful enough motivation to keep me from going overboard, and I actually lost a few pounds during that cruise, mostly because I ratcheted up my physical activity. I still enjoyed a lot of delicious food but balanced it out with increased exercise.

My appearance on *Today* was an exciting experience, although it seemed to be over very quickly. Due to work obligations, I couldn't spend any extra time in New York. I flew into LaGuardia and was met by *Today's* limousine driver who took me to my hotel directly across the street from Rockefeller Center. My friend Lee also flew in from Ohio and was able to be with me on the set.

I was scheduled to appear during the later hour of *Today*, with Kathy Lee Gifford and Hoda Kotb. I had high hopes of meeting some of the other early morning hosts, and I wasn't disappointed. As we waited in the hallway to go on camera, Meredith Viera walked out of her dressing room. Joy told her about me, and she congratulated me and gave me a big hug. I thought she was a very genuine and classy lady.

Prior to that moment, I had been holed up in what is known as the green room. Most television news programs have a green room, and no one is sure where the idea/concept came from. The room is genuinely painted green, and it's the location where guests wait their turn to appear on their segment of the show. It's also the location where non-famous folks such as me have the best chance of interacting with famous folks.

The first famous person I encountered (after Joy Bauer) was just outside the green room. Before entering, I spent a few moments in a make-up chair and sitting next to me was Jillian Michaels, who at that time was on *The Biggest Loser*. We had an opportunity to chat for about five minutes. She congratulated me on my success, provided some tips about what to do about extra skin, gave me a big hug, and allowed me to snap a photo. I thought she was very kind and genuine as well.

She's also very petite, which surprised me. Having watched her on *The Biggest Loser*, I had imagined she had a large and dominating body type. She's definitely very muscular but is quite petite otherwise. It just goes to show that what we see on camera isn't always completely accurate.

Once I entered the green room, I found myself with two other celebrities. I don't recall the name of the first guy. He was some English dude who specialized in fancy dinner etiquette. His segment, which happened before mine, had to do with designing a fancy table setting for a particular event.

The other person in the green room really caught my attention. Sitting next to me on the couch was Miss America, who had been crowned the evening before. Katie Stam, Miss Indiana, was kind, down to earth, and knew a lot about Michigan. She had a brother who attended Michigan State University and was well aware of the layout of my area of the Mitten. We talked for several minutes, posed for some pictures, and had a nice time interacting and discussing our Midwest roots and values.

One of my friends asked me if I asked for her phone number. I scoffed and asked him if he was crazy. Deep down, I was still that ugly person I had been my entire life and the thought of trying to score a date with Miss America never even entered my mind whatsoever.

The actual segment that morning focused on my success with The LIFE Diet®, with a visual aid related to my former eating habits. Hanging behind my head were a couple pairs of my former pants. A stack of a dozen Krispy Kreme donuts sat on the counter in front of me as an example of my former breakfast choices. I was excited, but not nervous. I had been on TV before, although not on a national program such as *Today*.

I was used to the bright lights of the camera and knew it was best to just have a conversation as if the camera wasn't even there. I was a bit distracted by the Kung Fu chef on the set right next to us who was busily preparing items in his wok for the next segment, but other than that, I felt calm and just enjoyed the dialogue.

When the segment was finished, Hoda Kotb shook my hand and congratulated me and quickly exited for the next segment. Kathy Lee Gifford grabbed my hand, looked me in the eye, and said, "God's going to use you to help many people." I have never forgotten that, and during the moments when I have felt like I have no hope or have nothing to offer, I have reminded myself of her words. Joy Bauer and the producer were very pleased and commented on how well I had done. I mumbled something about having been on TV before, but the producer told me she was extremely impressed and that I did much better than a lot of other people who appear on TV infrequently.

Apparently, I did well enough that Joy Bauer wanted to have me join her again, because a few months later, Joy and I appeared together on *The 700 Club* – the main news program of the Christian Broadcasting Network (CBN). This involved a trip to Virginia Beach, Virginia, and a much longer interview including detailed discussion of my former and current eating habits.

Jodi and Joy have both become lifelong friends and have continued to be an important source of encouragement and support. I have lost track of how many events Jodi and I did together in Michigan, but each one of them was powerful and energizing as we were able to share from our hearts, while also bringing the male/female perspective to discussions about weight. Believe it or not, men and women think about weight differently and have different experiences when it comes to how society treats them due to being overweight. Working together, Jodi and I were able to address co-ed audiences in a more effective manner than we could just on our own.

I am so grateful to Joy Bauer for her friendship. I assumed that after my moment in the spotlight, I would likely no longer be part of her circle of friends, but I was wrong. Joy cares about people and has reached out to see how I am doing on more than one occasion and often sends me birthday greetings. She also responds quickly to just about any question I have and has continued to answer my questions about diet and nutrition.

I am so thankful for the fellowship of both Jodi and Joy. I am thankful for their friendship and that neither one has given up on me even with the struggles and the swings I have faced since those early years of our interactions together. From the bottom of my heart, I want to say thank you to these two wonderful ladies.

I hope I am able to cultivate even an iota of the legacy the two of you have cultivated and continue to cultivate in the lives of the thousands of people you inspire and encourage each and every day.

I chose to make this "Inspiration" chapter the last for a reason: It's always best to end on a high note, right? I also wanted to leave you with positive thoughts and a hopeful outlook. Parts of this book have been hilarious. Parts of it have been sanguine. Parts of it have been sad. Parts of it have been difficult and negative. Those parts all add up together to one thing: my life, and probably mirror parts of your life, too. I started out by saying I was going to be real. Every single part I just mentioned is reality. Life is good, life is bad, life is happy, life is sad – that's just the nature of life.

As you know by now, I spent several years on the inspirational/motivational speaking circuit and did a lot of writing during that time. I loved the positive energy that developed as I talked with crowds large and small about changing my life, overcoming challenges, making healthy choices, and inspiring and encouraging others to do the same. It was powerful medicine for my own soul. I have come to discover great joy in giving my life and my story to people as a gift to help them overcome their own weight challenges.

As you also know by now, I've been on the dreaded yo-yo, just like many of you or many of those whom you love. Of course, I told myself I would not gain back the weight, and I live every day trying to make good choices that will lead to health and joyful living. But I'm human, and I have flaws and struggles – just like you do. Learning to forgive myself and to keep trying no matter what has been an important and life-altering decision.

I often began my interactions with an audience by telling them I'm just a normal, everyday guy who has a major weight problem. Although I often feel like I have somehow been cursed with the plague of obesity, the reality is I am just like everyone else in this world. My successes mean that everyone else in this world can be successful, too. I have refused to lie and say that it will be easy. It won't be. Moments of time in yo-yo hell may come along. Long and exhausting efforts to deal with emotional pain that is likely the root cause of an obesity problem will probably be necessary. But here's the good news:

YOU CAN DO IT! NEVER GIVE UP!

I live by those two phrases and keep them in front of me at all times. I repeat them to myself and to others whenever I have an opportunity. Why? Because it's true. You CAN do it. No matter where you find yourself, NEVER give up. There is always hope, so long as we keep the door ajar, even if it's ever so slightly, to give hope an opportunity to find its way into our hearts and lives.

About the Author

Jon Stanton lives in Sarasota, Florida, with his wife, Janet, and their two cats, Triscuit and Wheatabix.

Jon has a degree in communications from Siena Heights University in Adrian, Michigan. He also studied church music at Great Lakes Christian College in Lansing, Michigan, and Secondary Education with a major in English and a minor in History at Baker College in Owosso, Michigan.

Jon began his career serving as an administrative assistant and Director of Communications for the Health Care Association of Michigan, the state's largest trade association for long-term care facilities. He then spent ten years as Director of Administration and Communications for a public policy think tank based in Lansing.

After moving to Nebraska in 2012, Jon served as the start-up Executive Director for Dove's Nest, an Anabaptist organization focused on assisting faith communities with child protection issues and also worked for the University of Nebraska at Omaha.

Moving to Florida in 2017, Jon was the Creative Content Coordinator in the Communications and Marketing department at State College of Florida, Manatee-Sarasota, before pursuing a career as an author.

Jon loves to tell stories. His friends will vouch for that! He enjoys spending time in nature, with a special affinity for the birds and wildlife unique to Florida. He also loves music, especially sacred, classical, and four-part harmony.

Jon blogs regularly at HopeForTheHeavy.com. Visit his website, and signup to receive notices and information about future writing endeavors.

Made in the USA
Lexington, KY
21 November 2019